SABOTAGE

D1453541

SABOTAGE

LEADERSHIP THAT OVERCOMES BETRAYAL, THEFT AND DECEIT

BRANDON WILSON, APR

Propellor Company

Sabotage: Leadership That Overcomes Betrayal, Theft and Deceit

Copyright © 2021 Propellor Company

All rights reserved. No part of this publication may be reproduced, distributed, or transmitted in any form or by any means, including photocopying, recording, or other electronic or mechanical methods, without the prior written permission of the publisher, except in the case of brief quotations embodied in critical reviews and certain other noncommercial uses permitted by copyright law.

Published by Propellor Company
2101 6th Avenue North
Birmingham, Alabama 35203

United States

ISBN: 978-1-7373696-0-8

Cover design provided by Ford Wiles
Book editing provided by Vivian Roberson Syroyezhkin
Book interior design provided by Adina Cucicov

For Kenny B.
This is a work of love given to me
by God for you, my daughter.

To Shani, my incredible wife

Special Tribute: Bishop E. Good

"If your giftedness is greater than your character, then your character will hold down your giftedness."

—JOHN MAXWELL

CONTENTS

EPIGRAPH

Airplanes require a clear runway to generate the speed and momentum necessary for flight. Similarly, leaders need a clear path to generate the strength and confidence necessary to unlock their fullest potential along their journey.

May this book clear your leadership runway so that your bold ideas and purpose take flight.

A greater life and a better world for you—and those you serve—is at stake.

LET THE LEADING BEGIN

L ike many leaders, Maurice and Richard McDonald never saw their sabotage coming. At the time, preparing to protect themselves against sabotage wasn't their top leadership priority. When it became a priority, it was too late.

Maurice and Richard had other priorities, and big ones at that. These two pioneering brothers had set out to do more than build a new company. They wanted to change an entire industry.

Their industrious company was aptly named to tribute their family. They called their new company McDonald's.

Establishing McDonald's as a company that would redefine the entire quick-serve industry consumed all of their attention and focus. And their thoughtful execution and leadership was paying off.

However, Maurice and Richard's failure to prioritize defending their leadership pursuits against sabotage left them exposed. That leadership vulnerability was about to be attacked by a milkshake machine salesman named Ray Kroc.

Today, Ray Kroc—not Maurice and Richard—is the name people think of in relation to the founding of McDonald's, one of the most valuable brands in the world.

Using an aggressive blend of betrayal, theft and deceit, Kroc used his new relationship with the McDonald brothers to take their company, and eventually their legacy, as his own.

In all facets of his life, Kroc's powerful ambition compelled him to run through, over or around anyone who stood in the way of getting what he wanted. His ambition drove him, as opposed to him driving it.

Kroc, then a fifty-year-old with a declining milkshake machine sales business, met the McDonald brothers while filling a machine order. He was curious as to why someone would need as many milkshake machines as they did, but then, he saw the long lines at their restaurant and understood.

He learned that Maurice and Richard had built a cost-effective system for taking orders and making burgers and fries in a manner that reduced wasted motion—a process that, once perfected, would revolutionize the quick-serve restaurant industry.

When Kroc was filling that milkshake machine order, he did more than meet Maurice and Richard. He met something he wanted for himself.

Kroc wanted to actually become the McDonald brothers. To do this, he had only one thing in mind: take their innovation and their name.

After meeting the brothers, he convinced them to take him behind the curtain to show him the operations. Kroc took detailed notes, applauding the brothers for their innovative thinking and approach. He offered himself up as an employee to ingratiate himself with the brothers and gain their trust.

Kroc became responsible for selling McDonald's franchises across the country. While the McDonald brothers had started to expand a little, Kroc saw how much money he could potentially make doing this and moved to put a McDonald's restaurant everywhere he could.

The deal Kroc made with the brothers leaned heavily in his own favor—he received 1.9% of all gross sales for every franchise he sold, and Maurice and Richard only received 0.5%. Despite creating eighteen more locations in one year, Kroc wanted more. His ambition wasn't satisfied.

Per the advisement of a clever business consultant, Henry Sorbonne, Kroc uncovered that the best way to make money off the McDonald's brand wasn't through selling burgers, but through buying the real estate the restaurants sat on.

Seeing an opportunity, Kroc founded a real estate company, not a restaurant. He then used said company to stealthily enrich himself. He became the landlord to every franchisee, so he was guaranteed to make money no matter what the franchise's sales were.

But still, his overreaching ambition couldn't be satisfied and his callousness for the McDonalds grew.

They clashed over the direction of the company, with Kroc taking a more aggressive approach. Kroc wasn't able to make the changes that could make him even richer, so he made them a deal that ultimately sabotaged the brothers' financial futures and legacy.

Kroc bought the company outright for a little less than three million dollars and walked back his commitment to pay the brothers a royalty in perpetuity. By then, the franchises were pulling in fifty-six million dollars a year. If Kroc had kept paying them a royalty, the brothers would have received fifteen million dollars a year by 1977, the equivalent of more than sixty-three million dollars today.

However, this sale didn't include the original McDonald's location, to Kroc's fury. As he said to a long-time employee, "I'm not normally a vindictive man, but this time I'm going to get those sons-of-bitches."

Kroc then opened up a McDonald's restaurant across the street from the original, forcing the brothers to change the restaurant's name. It closed six months later. As Kroc said happily to *TIME*, "I ran 'em out of business."

In a final act of betrayal, he moved to erase them from history for his own gain. He put busts of himself in every store and celebrated himself on the company's Founder's Day. The true founders were only recognized as such in 1991, thirty years after they sold the company to Kroc.

In an interview with The Daily Mail Online, the McDonald brothers' nephew, Ronald McDonald, said, "It was all ego. Ray Kroc just wanted more and more. Name me one other American corporation where an employee became the founder."

The McDonald brothers were sabotaged. They never saw it coming. As a result, they were unable to protect their pursuits or their financial stake in the company they founded. Today, McDonald's is valued at twenty-five billion dollars, and is one of the world's most valuable brands.

As leaders, we have a lot in common with Maurice and Richard. We establish a vision, set a goal and pursue it with vigor. We lead with enterprise and diligence, just like they did. However, Maurice and Richard's leadership journey is a cautionary tale. If we fail to prioritize protecting our leadership from sabotage, we risk having our vision taken away by someone else.

A leader's ability to discern whether or not others support their leadership, vision and priorities is a monumental—and deeply undervalued—leadership skill.

This discernment is the hallmark of leaders who execute their large and audacious pursuits with seemingly little resistance. These are the leaders we consider highly effective and wise. These are the leaders who become the stuff of lore.

Consider Steve Jobs' leadership journey. His prolific contributions to technology and design would have never come to fruition if he lacked the ability to identify, conquer and survive sabotage. If other Apple executives and board members had their way, the world might not have received the iPhone.

Jobs' superpower was his ability to recognize those who believed in his vision, and most importantly, those who didn't.

In 1980, Jobs took Apple public while serving as CEO. The momentum he garnered from this move propelled Apple into the ranks of the Fortune 500. Jobs hired John Sculley from Pepsi Co. to serve as Apple's chief executive—a move that would allow Jobs to work closely with developers to launch Apple's most revolutionary product to date: the Macintosh (Mac) computer. When the Mac debuted in 1984 the reviews were great. The sales were not.

Sculley used this fact as ammunition to end a long-standing and intense power struggle he had with Jobs. Sculley, seeking to focus on stability rather than innovation, convinced the board that Jobs was out of control and in over his head. The board agreed and stripped Jobs of his managerial responsibilities, and authority. Jobs was relegated to an office with a set of obscure and unimportant responsibilities, essentially getting pushed out of the company he co-founded.

Jobs used one word to describe what Sculley did to him: betrayal. He never forgave Sculley for what he did before his passing.

The next chapters of Jobs' life and leadership were defined by his ability to survive Sculley's sabotage and become a leader determined to protect his future pursuits from betrayal, theft and deceit.

As a result of this rarely documented leadership skill, we know Apple today as an engine of innovation that's using technology and design to shape the way we engage with each other and the world.

Now imagine what Apple would be like today if the company were nurtured and grown by Sculley—a former Pepsi Co. executive. I'd bet that it would be a completely different company than the one envisioned by Steve Jobs.

Conversely, imagine what McDonald's would be today had it become the company envisioned by two brothers who worked as Hollywood movie set designers. I'd bet that company would be wholly different than the one we know today. Instead, McDonald's is a company that resembles the vision of a real estate mogul.

The difference between Steve Jobs and the McDonald brothers—and the reason we ponder the legacy of one and not the others—is that Steve possessed the leadership skills necessary to overcome sabotage.

Today, after nearly twenty years as a communications professional, I am the founder of an advertising agency, a developer of leaders and a communications consultant to executives of several organizations, including Fortune 500 companies. My leadership has impacted some of the most prominent brands in the world, including Honda, Pfizer, Verizon Wireless and others. I have also helped the presidents at more than a hundred colleges and universities navigate major crises and on-campus violence.

However, despite the intense exposure to leadership calamity and crisis I've had in my career, nothing has prepared me more for understanding sabotage than being one of its victims.

To understand the stakes of my battle with sabotage, it is important to know that as a youth, my family and I never had much. We were happy but poor, and once that poverty led to a brief stint of homelessness.

Despite these circumstances, I studied hard, obeyed the law and prayed often. Although it was difficult to imagine myself as a business owner and influencer to leaders, I wanted to be ready if I had the opportunity to improve my life and the lives of those I loved.

The opportunity came from an unlikely source. A very powerful civil rights attorney sent a message through a proxy that he was interested in investing in me. I received the phone call while working in a call center that sold carpet cleaning services.

As an aside, some of the most pivotal moments in my life happened when I was at my most vulnerable. As a homeless teenager, I received acceptance to the only college I applied to, Auburn University. My strange encounters with opportunity made me believe in the power of vulnerability, and helped me start expecting that incredible things were about to happen when I was at my lowest.

Now, standing in the break room of a carpet cleaning company, holding a phone that was days from being deactivated, I was receiving an opportunity of a lifetime. I couldn't believe my ears.

The voice on the other end of the phone wanted me to start a division at the civil rights attorney's organization dedicated to providing presidents at universities with strategies for making their campuses more inclusive and diverse. I was twenty-four years old and scared to death.

I had no other choice. I accepted the challenge.

This work exposed me to leaders from every corner of the country and provided me access to powerful mentors. These mentors poured their confidence and belief in me. They also encouraged me to start my own company—something a poor kid from the wrong side of tracks never believed he could do.

I took the leap. I invested in myself and started my own advertising and communications agency. To my surprise, the company took off like a rocket. Before long, I was making enough money to help my family and provide jobs to those in need. I had also earned enough money to begin seriously thinking about acquiring other companies to expand my business and influence. It wasn't long before I started making plans to start my own family.

It was at this point—the moment I dared to cash in my skills and confidence for millions of dollars—that agents of sabotage started to take note.

My agent of sabotage was a bully and he wanted everything I'd gained from my unlikely climb from poverty. He had a client list worth millions of dollars, so when he called, I picked up the phone.

I should have let the phone call go unanswered.

This cunning agent of sabotage never wanted to sell me his business. His ruse cleverly drew me into his web, and he developed a relationship with me that can best be described as uneven. In short, he wielded his influence to convincingly intimidate me into giving him what he wanted. I caved.

Years later, when I was nearly out of money, I found the courage to put an end to his sabotage. I stood up to my bully.

When I rejected his attempts to control me, my agent of sabotage responded with force and threats. After an ugly, long and expensive battle—and nearly $700,000 later—I survived.

My clients refused to abandon me. My criminal defense attorney proved my agent of sabotage was running the sham. My employees stuck it out. And most importantly, my wife remained at my side. Today we have a wonderful daughter, Kenny Wilson, and my company is thriving in ways I'd never imagined.

When faced with sabotage, my mentors were of little help. Many of them had never started a company that merged with or acquired another company. They also mostly held powerful salaried positions at influential companies.

The authors of bestselling books were also of little help. Although many of their books offered great insights about leadership and business management, very few—if any—provided any insights that were helpful for surviving sabotage.

During my battle with sabotage, I was alone and in over my head. My most formidable weapons were prayer and the occasional stroke of luck.

This feeling of loneliness compelled me to write this book. My hope is that it becomes a companion resource to any leader being confronted with sabotage.

Although I lost a ton of money, my battle with sabotage provided me unprecedented understanding of the behaviors of sabotage. Instead of lamenting the experience, I studied it. I interviewed other leaders and studied their bouts with sabotage. I developed a deep appreciation for how pervasive sabotage is in our lives, and how woefully unprepared leaders are to confront it.

In these pages are nearly twenty years of leadership wisdom for understanding sabotage, the biggest enemy to your leadership effectiveness. The wisdom in this book contains lessons that many leaders only gain though painful trial and error. It is being offered to you via the comforts of your desk, reading room or car.

This book will prepare you to achieve the next level of leadership in your life. It will equip you with the keys needed to unlock new levels of effectiveness. It will prepare you to achieve your best life, unencumbered by betrayal, theft and deceit.

The stakes are extremely high for everyone from chief executives of corporations to founders of startups, to other leaders in between.

Whether you want to change an entire industry like the McDonald brothers or transform the way we experience the world like Steve Jobs, there is much depending on your leadership. Don't let sabotage deny you or the world from realizing the gifts of your leadership journey.

To leaders everywhere, these chapters are a start to your journey to becoming one of the greats. These are the tools needed to inspire incredible change while thwarting the forces that seek to steal, betray and stymie your success.

Let the leading begin.

UNDERSTANDING WHAT
DRIVES PEOPLE
TO SABOTAGE

———

CHAPTER ONE

WHAT IS SABOTAGE?

N o one wants to admit it, let alone write a book about it, but sabotage is all around us. We all know how it looks, how it feels, and how it can impact lives. However, many people are ill-prepared for its attack. Even fewer know how to survive or overcome it.

Sabotage is in every corporation in the world—even the most beloved. From Facebook to Wells Fargo to companies in between, there are countless stories of betrayal, theft and deceit.

Then there is the sabotage that happens in our personal lives. These acts of sabotage cause havoc to personal and business relationships, and undermine our leadership pursuits. These attacks can damage our reputations, and in the process, sink the leadership endeavors and pursuits we've worked diligently to execute.

We read about these acts and hear about them from friends. But, very rarely are we provided the tools to ward off these potent and selfish attacks before they strike.

Surprisingly, as pervasive as sabotage is in every aspect of life, many cannot clearly state what it is. If you were to ask ten people to define the term, many of them would struggle to string together the words to succinctly describe it.

Sabotage is any activity that seeks to obstruct, disrupt or destroy someone else for selfish gain. In the context of this book, sabotage aims to do this to our leadership, and our leadership pursuits.

Using theft, betrayal and deceit as its weaponry, sabotage targets organizations, people, relationships, endeavors, operations, systems and practices.

When people try to sabotage leaders they will often operate with guile and subversion. And, their motivation will be one or more of the following: jealousy, lying, arrogance, or seduction.

The following hypothetical scenario provides a glimpse into how all of the classic attributes of sabotage can work together to undermine and destroy a leader's pursuit.

In this case, a well-respected and diligent FBI agent investigates potential criminal activity in a group of people. The group being investigated is diverse, which allows each member to have a role in carrying out the alleged criminal activity.

As the investigation takes shape, one of the suspects defects from the criminal coalition and cooperates with the investigation. In exchange for his cooperation, the FBI agrees to a plea deal that details the extent of the alleged criminals' relationships with each other and outlines expectations for truth, transparency and cooperation.

However, there is one small detail that's not obvious when the deal is made and executed: The suspect who claimed to defect and cooperate with investigators never planned to do so at all.

The suspect feigned cooperation to infiltrate the investigation, steal its details, and share them with the criminal coalition to help them prepare to defeat the case being made against them.

This is a great case study for understanding what an act of sabotage looks like, as it contains the three behaviors that consistently appear when sabotage is present:

Guile: Guile is sly or cunning intelligence. Those who master guile do so with practice, forethought and a craftiness that allows elusion.

Subversion: Subversion is the deliberate undermining of authority to destabilize or ruin the order of things. There will always be an attempt to gain entry into its targets circles—be it through trust or acceptance of authority. Once the agent of sabotage gains entry, they then position themselves to be a disturbing force to the operations and practices of the institution.

Personal Benefit: The person conducting the sabotage will seek to obtain a selfish advantage, benefit or thing of value at some point. They often want to flee the damage they've caused, escape retribution, overthrow the targeted authority, or execute a coup to replace the victims of their sabotage.

These three behaviors work together to obstruct, disrupt, and destroy their target.

Being able to discern the motivations that drive people to sabotage is a key leadership skill to survive and ultimately avoid it. Each of these motivations take the form of the Four Horsemen of Sabotage.

THE FOUR HORSEMEN OF SABOTAGE

As sabotage moves about within our lives and our organizations, it does so clothed in elusion. Agents of sabotage are often masters at blending in, using others to shield them from accountability, or falsely operating as trusted advisers to leaders—striking before any defense can stop them.

In all cases of a sabotage, whether the operative blends in, uses others to avoid accountability, or leverages their position as a trusted adviser to disguise ill intent, what you see is not what you get.

To develop the skills needed to identify, address and remove the potential for sabotage in your life, I encourage leaders to look for evidence of the Four Horsemen of Sabotage. These Horsemen are the motivations that those wishing to sabotage us use to justify their attacks on our lives and leadership.

We will further dissect each horseman in later chapters, but note that sometimes to find these Horsemen, leaders need only to look within. Sabotage is a two-way street. Yes, sabotage can happen to us, but we can also exact sabotage on others. If we are not vigilant, these Horsemen could also impact the way we treat others along our journeys to achieving our best life and leadership.

Each horseman carries the following name:

Jealousy

Jealousy is hatred disguised as anything but. People who are filled with jealousy are driven to be divisive and serve as authors of discord. They are driven by contention and triggered by competition.

When searching your life or those around you for the presence of jealousy, there are a few areas to monitor. They include one's appetite for competition. If you or those in your network are compelled to seek extreme—and at times unethical—measures to win, this horseman might be at work. Another red flag involves an insatiable appetite to elevate oneself at the expense of others. They might want to literally have what you've earned or even become a version of you.

Lying

Liars are masters of deception. So much so that extreme cases even compel those compromised by this horseman to deceive themselves into believing and justifying their deceitful ways.

Monitoring your susceptibility to lying, or its presence in and around your life, requires that you gauge one's penchant for being accusatory. Throwing others under the proverbial bus to dodge accountability is a classic tactic of people consumed with lying. Accountability lives in truth. These operatives of sabotage don't.

Arrogance

Arrogance, or haughtiness, revels in rebellion. It presents itself as an inability to be coached or taught, or as defiance. As managers, people who are haughty will shun professional development and stubbornly remain anchored in their own opinions despite evidence to the contrary.

The pride that accompanies arrogance is not an enabling force, but one that disables one's ability to self-correct or cease wrongdoing once it's known. This pride makes it difficult for the operative to avoid becoming a repeat offender of sabotage.

Arrogance also shows itself as a disregard for others, shown through either unrestrained ambition, bullying, or acts of revenge. The callousness that comes with haughtiness makes it easy for these agents of sabotage to hurt or destroy with little regard for others.

Arrogance frequently ensnares leaders themselves. As a by-product, arrogant leaders are not self-aware and lack the emotional intelligence needed to be sensitive to the impact that their actions have on others.

Seduction

These agents of sabotage usually operate behind false fronts, using flattery to obtain positions of influence or become advisers in the lives and organizations of those they seek to sabotage. As a weapon, flattery attempts to distract unassuming victims of sabotage from the malice at hand, causing them to bring down their defenses by appealing to our need to feel valued.

Those driven by this horseman also reveal themselves by always pointing to alternative methods—sometimes questionable ones at that—for achieving desired ends. They believe that the ends are always justified, regardless of the means, and find joy in convincing you to go along for the ride.

— — —

Taken together, these Horsemen provide leaders with the signs they need to gauge their susceptibility to sabotage. As leaders, we've already encountered one or all four of these Horsemen within our lives. But viewing them as an early signal of sabotage will help reduce your exposure to its presence and impact in your life.

Lining the shelves of bookstores are books about best leadership practices. They are all informative, but most of them are incomplete at best. They fail to prepare you to survive the proverbial spook on the other side of the door waiting to trip you up on the way to executing an amazingly worthwhile project.

Leadership is hard by itself. Without the skills needed to thwart the well-laid plans of agents of sabotage, luck is often the best defense for leaders who wish to thrive and succeed.

There is, however, a brand of leaders that shuns luck. These leaders instead develop a reliance on the skills needed to survive sabotage, and thrive even in its midst. This brand of leaders understands a vital point: surviving sabotage can mean the difference between success and failure.

THE BRIEF

Sabotage is any activity that seeks to obstruct, disrupt or destroy someone else for selfish gain. In the context of this book, sabotage aims to do this to our leadership and our leadership pursuits.

Three behaviors consistently appear when sabotage is present:

1. Guile: A sly or cunning intelligence
2. Subversion: The deliberate undermining of authority to destabilize or ruin the order of things.
3. Personal benefit: The person conducting sabotage will try to obtain a selfish advantage, benefit, or thing of value.

The motivations for sabotage take the form of the Four Horsemen of Sabotage:

1. Jealousy
2. Lying
3. Arrogance
4. Seduction

Paying attention to signs of each of these Horsemen will equip you to fight sabotage.

CHAPTER TWO

SURVIVING SABOTAGE IS A HIGH STAKES EXERCISE FOR LEADERS

As I mentioned in the first chapter, people often have a hard time clearly defining sabotage. The same can be said of understanding just how devastating and pervasive it can be to leaders and their pursuits.

To understand why sabotage is so significant to succeeding as a leader, we can look at the rise and fall of Aaron Beam.

Beam was the co-founder and former CFO of HealthSouth, the nation's first orthopedic rehabilitation chain of hospitals. HealthSouth became a brand name for many, including celebrity athletes like Michael Jordan and Charles Barkley.

Unfortunately for Beam, his co-founder, Richard Scrushy was a skilled agent of sabotage. He used various methods to win the loyalty of talented employees, only to betray them once he received what he was after.

Rumor has it that Scrushy carried a firearm in his briefcase. Those in his immediate circle believed he was capable of violence. As a leader, Scrushy has been described as incredibly mercurial. He intimidated his employees. He used company-wide meetings to embarrass those who sought to defy him. He even installed cameras across the company to surveil every move of those who worked for him.

In an interview with CFO.com, Beam corroborates this account:

"Unless you were there and experienced it, it's hard to understand. You couldn't tell [Scrushy] no on anything. I have seen him so mad over minor things that I actually feared for my physical safety."

The meeting with Scrushy in the summer of 1996 would be one of those encounters.

Upon sharing the news that HealthSouth had missed its earnings projections, Beam said Scrushy turned red and began trembling. He aggressively admonished Beam, and said that reporting bad numbers would bring an end to Beam being a "rock star." The message was clear—fix it, or else.

Beam lacked the skills needed to stop the sabotage Scrushy was inflicting on everyone around him. Beam caved, choosing instead to participate in what would become a multi-billion dollar accounting fraud.

Beam and five other CFOs from HealthSouth would plead guilty to criminal charges. Aaron would lose his wealth, including his three million dollar home, and become a convicted felon.

Today he lives a quiet life in Loxley, Alabama, where he manages a grass cutting business—a far cry from the lifestyle he was living before.

Scrushy's actions took more than just money or freedom from Beam. As an agent of sabotage, Scrushy attacked three things that are vital to good leadership: making decisions, creating transformative change, and maintaining a growth mindset. Once these leadership skills were compromised, Beam could no longer operate in leadership.

For any leader, having these three leadership skills compromised results in an inability to effectively lead. Here's how:

SABOTAGE STEALS A LEADER'S ABILITY TO MAKE DECISIONS

Leadership is simply having the power to make a decision. This power is exactly what sabotage is after whenever it strikes.

When sabotage strikes a person's life, it steals their will to have a better life. When sabotage strikes a pursuit, it robs the leader of the ability to seek better for those they lead. Finally, when sabotage strikes an organization, it attempts to frustrate the leader and weaken their will to innovate for the future.

The greatest and wisest leaders of our time have developed a mentality that provides them the audacity, courage and independence to make decisions that impact their present situation or circumstances.

Developing this mentality is not easy. As a matter of fact, it can be downright painful. Some of the decisions these leaders have made along the way have led to great loss, inconvenience, suffering and even displacement. But in those times, these leaders learn precious lessons in accountability. Leaders become great when they survive these circumstances and still believe in the power of decision.

Having the authority to make a decision requires the development of the three characteristics I previously mentioned: Audacity, independence and courage. Those who want to steal a leader's ability to be effective sabotage their ability to do so by attacking one or each of these three characteristics.

One such instance was a negotiation I witnessed between board members for a park and its large landowner. In renewing the management agreement that guided the relationship between the park's board and the landowner, the leaders of the board realized that the landowner retained massive negotiation leverage by virtue of ownership.

As a result, some of the terms proposed and tactics deployed by the landowner undermined their attempts at fair dealings and transparency. As time wore on, the urgency rose to finalize negotiations for the sake of employees that could be impacted. The leaders felt they had little choice but to give in to the unfair terms.

Their attrition was the result of tactics deployed by the land owner to dull the leaders' audacity, independence and courage to be innovative problem solvers.

Agents of sabotage who will inevitably come into our lives fully understand that a leader without audacity, independence or courage is a leader who suffers a diminished will to make a decision.

At least that's the hope of the agent of sabotage.

Highly effective leaders guard the power of decision-making from sabotage. They never, and I mean never, sacrifice the strength needed to choose the kind of life they want for themselves.

SABOTAGE THWARTS TRANSFORMATION

As an employee, I've seen multiple cases where supervisors rush to superiors with lies that seek to assassinate the reputation of other managers within the company. The lies and misinformation were always attempts to diminish the manager's credibility, and ultimately cause them to be removed them from authority.

As a chief executive, I've experienced outright dishonesty from employees seeking to sabotage me personally—setting me up to be embarrassed before a major client. The skills detailed in this book helped me identify those attempts, and survive.

As a consultant to organizations, I've counseled other chief executives through attempts by those in their companies to create rogue power centers within their organizations that could weaken and usurp the authority of the CEO.

In each of these cases, regardless of the tactic, the objective was clear: to diminish the leader's ability to be effective when creating change.

When leaders seek major pursuits, their goals are much larger than the people involved. The pursuits also outweigh anything the agents of sabotage could ever hope to receive in return for their duplicity.

However, despite how minor or tangential the internal short-comings facing those who betray, they may scuttle a leader's entire pursuit if left unaddressed. When sabotage succeeds, everyone loses out on a chance to do and benefit from something great.

Whether you're a public official, a pastor, nonprofit director, entrepreneur, chief executive or school superintendent, people will inevitably find ways to make your journey to achieving transformation more challenging than it already is.

This is not a complaint. This is a reality that very few leaders are prepared to face. And as a result, leaders miss multiple opportunities to prepare to overcome sabotage and unlock the next levels of their leadership. This body of work meets each leader in that reality.

I have seen a number of sabotage attempts—some successful and others not—that tried to thwart leaders seeking to achieve the transformative. In each of the cases, the sabotage came from one of the many quadrants that impacts each of our lives: political, communal, familial, and social.

I witnessed how sabotage could come from numerous angles while working as a consultant to a faith-based university in the Midwest. I distinctly remember the struggles their leaders faced to make their campus community more diverse and inclusive.

I was commissioned to recommend ways to address and limit religious intolerance and violence against members of the indigenous and LGBTQ communities.

While on campus, I asked the leaders to assemble an audience of all the involved stakeholders for me—the culprits of discrimination and the targeted. What I didn't prepare for was walking into an auditorium filled with hundreds of students who felt justified in their right to offend other people. The session was intense and the insensitivities between the different groups in the room aptly reflected the culture of the campus community.

After that meeting, I met with the vice president of student affairs—a post empowered to implement my recommendations for unifying the campus and thwarting hate and bigotry. He was in a tough leadership position. His decisions had the chance to literally save students' lives and provide others with protection.

During our meeting, he shared the challenges he would face while trying to implement my recommendations.

He knew his fight would be with agents of sabotage from the city council, residents who belonged to his church, and school employees who wielded their faith as weapons of intolerance and discrimination. As background, the political climate—heavily influenced by the weaponizing of religion—had created a culture rout with intolerant acts against those perceived as not having biblical protection, and those who had historically been oppressed and isolated.

I challenged him, imploring that doing what's difficult must be done if it means saving a student's life and making a campus safer. This leader, who I have come to admire, did just that.

One year after our tough talk, I received a phone call. It was the vice president of student affairs. He called to share that he had successfully implemented each one of my recommendations.

His work to better the campus community unlocked sabotage from all corners—from political leaders, the community and within the university. With that, he shared that his work at the university was done, and that his fight with sabotage had been tough but well worth it. So much so that the only decision left for him to make in the wake of his transformative work was what college he would work for next.

He had sacrificed his job to make an entire campus community better, safer and more inclusive. Today, that campus is in a better place. So is his career.

The stakes for leaders are always high. That's precisely why sabotage seeks them out. Our ability to be transformative is always seen as a threat to complacency. Our ability to challenge norms makes us valuable enough to steal from and an affront to those who resist progress.

Surviving sabotage doesn't always mean that you will ride off into the sunset unscathed. Sometimes sacrifice is required. Having an ability to survive sabotage begins with the courage to lead despite this.

When the outcomes transform lives and communities, I dare say the journey is always worth it.

SABOTAGE CREATES A MENTALITY OF POVERTY

Effective leaders have a growth mindset. This mentality is defined in different ways, but the crux of it is the belief that one's actions and decisions have the ability to generate abundance, prosperity and difference. In short, leaders with a growth mindset are leaders of positive consequence.

Leaders who possess a growth mentality understand the value of always being intentional about their decisions to pursue greater. They know that when they dedicate their leadership to an effort, their very presence has the ability to generate expansion and growth—including increases to their own territory and influence. As a net benefit, leading with a growth mentality also inspires those you lead to be bold about their own leadership pursuits, while simultaneously helping you unlock the potential for the projects you are passionate about.

Becoming an effective leader with a growth mentality requires sustainability. It is not a moment. It is more than a short set of accomplishments. But rather, it's a lifestyle undergirded by a commitment to developing the wisdom needed to protect your pursuits from sabotage.

My career has exposed me to a number of leaders who had all of the ingredients to become effective leaders. These leaders start along their leadership journey with vigor and intention. They garner a few signature wins, but over time, they grow overly cautious, risk-averse and complacent. The result is always a leadership journey that stalls before ever reaching its destination.

The difficulty associated with becoming a leader of consequence who consistently delivers measurable impact is the result of one enemy: A mentality of poverty.

Poverty is elusive because we often think of poverty as someone else's problem when in fact, the thinking of all leaders is constantly at risk of being compromised by a mentality of poverty.

Poverty can plague leaders of all stripes—regardless one's net worth or life circumstances. Its most potent ability is diminishing a leader's drive to achieve greater in their life.

Understanding poverty, as a construct and mentality, requires an acute understanding of how it works. It convinces leaders that abundance and prosperity are bad things, making those leaders adopt a mentality of fear and lack.

Leaders who succumb to a mentality of poverty find themselves vulnerable to sabotage because it diminishes the leader's ability to establish a management culture that continues to advance.The stagnation it causes can make your organization—and life—susceptible to being targeted by deceit, theft and betrayal.

As an analogy, consider the constant software updates needed for your smart devices and computers. In order to operate optimally, these updates ensure that the algorithms and security tools that keep your devices safe are always in their most advanced state. This constant updating makes it difficult for your devices to be hacked by those who seek to corrupt your device and steal its contents.

As with our smart devices, the management cultures leaders establish in their organizations and the relationships they preserve in their personal lives must also operate in a constant state of improvement in order to thrive, remain relevant, and be advanced enough to make it difficult to be hacked by sabotage.

THE BRIEF

Sabotage compromises three necessary skills for effective leadership:

1. Sabotage steals a leader's ability to make decisions
2. Sabotage thwarts transformation
3. Sabotage creates a mentality of poverty

CHAPTER THREE

DISASSEMBLING THE POWER THAT DRIVES SABOTAGE

———————

C hoosing to be better, putting in the hard work, and leading with abundance in mind should lead to wealth, success, influence, and a better life. It also means becoming a target for betrayal, theft and deceit.

Armoring yourself against sabotage is not a matter of paranoia. It's a matter of wisdom. Leaders who understand what drives people to sabotage possess a competitive advantage in the work place, marketplace and in the politics of business management.

As prolific as sabotage is in all of our lives, I am amazed at the number of people who find themselves ill-prepared to recognize, thwart and respond to it when it strikes. Consequently, leaders' lack of preparedness and understanding of sabotage results in a lack of protection against its attacks.

So, what drives agents of sabotage? To become a more effective leader, it is enormously important to understand why people betray, deceive and steal.

There are eight things that drive people to sabotage. They include unfulfilled personal needs, a desire to act out the lives of others, a penchant for lying, a desire to correct a perceived wrong, callousness, overreaching ambition, resistance to accountability, and the desire to operate behind false fronts. You may notice that each of these can be categorized to align with the Four Horsemen we discussed previously.

Here is a deeper dive into each of these drivers for sabotage.

UNFULFILLED PERSONAL NEEDS

Some agents of sabotage betray others because of unmet character or emotional needs. Ray Kroc, the self-proclaimed founder of McDonald's, is a classic example of someone who betrayed to meet some unfulfilled personal need. His betrayal of the McDonald brothers was executed, among other reasons, because he saw them as a vehicle for achieving the kind of business success that had eluded him.

These agents of sabotage can be quite aggressive and calculating in their betrayal. Their attacks are often attempts to compensate for and hide, low self-efficacy, esteem or other internal weaknesses. If they felt that they could achieve goals on their own, they wouldn't resort to sabotage.

These agents of sabotage are often great students of their prey. They are well- planned and calculating—and will use every resource available to aggressively defend against the accusation of betrayal if caught to avoid having the weaknesses of their true personalities and emotions exposed.

A DESIRE TO ACT OUT THE LIVES OF OTHERS

These agents of sabotage usually live pretty mundane lives. They are at our places of work, in our networks and in our personal lives. They secretly desire your position at work or your family life, are jealous of your promotions, want to be the chief executive, or are angry that their career is not advancing quickly enough.

Agents of sabotage who act out the lives of others generally fall into the category of con artists. But contrary to television portrayal of con artists as exciting, high-flying people, the reality is a lot more mundane. They are driven by short-term and intermediate goals. They enter our lives for a season, or just in time to obtain a certain treasure.

These agents also take on the personas of others as much as they prey on them for their valuable physical possessions. This doesn't necessarily mean stealing one's identity, but it could include basking in the perceived limelight or inner circles of influence of those they prey upon.

Instead of having their grievances heard, they study. They study how to become your friend, your spouse, your resource and your confidant. Once they collect enough intelligence, they act to dispose of their prey—throwing them under the bus in ways that ensure professional or personal demise, or allow them to assume the lifestyle of their victim.

LIARS

At its core, lying is knowingly and willfully speaking falsehoods, and doing so with intent. Sometimes the intent is to simply convince oneself that what they did or didn't do was justifiable. In other cases, it convinces the wrongdoer that something didn't happen, even though they participated in or knowingly did a certain act.

As an example, think of a child with chocolate stains around their mouth as they say, "I didn't eat any chocolate." Lying habitually in the small things has the effect of dropping a ton of feathers. Put together, they weigh a lot. Small lies are actually quite big, because they show a proclivity to deceive others to achieve a selfish end.

Even when the act of lying hasn't become habitual, it attacks the trust needed to build and sustain productive relationships. It disadvantages other parties in the relationship by causing them to make decisions without complete or adequate information.

An advanced and malicious form of lying involves lying to harm others. While we mostly think about lying as a selfish attempt to elude accountability, liars can also intentionally harm others to save themselves. Lying to harm others is amazingly reckless. These liars weaponize lying for self-preservation, and with little regard of the impact or harm it poses to others.

In all cases, lying is a behavior that's embraced by most agents of sabotage. The behavior communicates a few things that embody the classic tenets of deception and guile. It shows that the liar does not want to be the subject of focus. This is anchored by a desire to operate undetected or questioned. It communicates self-absorption, which is driven by a desire to think of yourself first, even at the expense of others. And, it communicates that they are willing to harm others to preserve themselves.

A DESIRE TO CORRECT A PERCEIVED WRONG

Some agents of sabotage convince themselves that their sabotage is actually an act of altruism. They're motivated by a relentless drive to do things better and accomplish more than their victims. At work, they study the processes and procedures of the culture, meticulously take notes on the training and professional development practices, and stash away documents and client contacts "in the event" they need them one day.

As they lie, they tell themselves that if this were their corporation they'd do things differently. If this were their company, they'd treat clients better. And, if they made the kind of money such-and-such made, they'd invest it in this and that way.

That drive to correct the perceived wrongs or inadequate business practices of others is just the fuel they need to justify acts like: using company time to recruit other employees to leave with them to start other ventures, poaching clients, redirecting money from their employers for initiatives that essentially fund their personal agendas, and hijacking the processes of another place as their own.

At other times, the agent's wrongdoing is personal. They simply feel that a place is pigeonholing them, denying them progress or overlooking them and others. In either case, they liken their activity to that of a superhero who swoops down to save the collective interests of others, and advance their own priorities in the process.

Because their choice to betray tries to "help," they feel justified in their wrongdoing and guile. Judas is an example of this kind of agent of sabotage. He convinced himself that there was a better way to establish the Kingdom on Earth, and constantly clashed with Jesus' ways and instructions.

He also, over time, tried to indoctrinate other disciples and imposed questionable financial practices to justify his own needs—even stealing when the opportunity presented itself. Handing Jesus over to the Sanhedrin—in Judas' mind—was likely his way of undoing perceived wrongs associated with his disagreements with Jesus' philosophies. Those "wrongs" consumed his mind, and drove him to betray.

CALLOUSNESS

These agents of sabotage are ruthless, cold and abusive. Their callousness can be expressed as bullying, unfair dealing or suppression. In any form, the objective is always clear to its targets: their bully wants to make them too afraid to do anything to exercise your own independence.

Those who operate with callousness consider influence and fear their superpowers. Their influence is often used to recruit others to do their bidding to create a level of separation between themselves and their targets of sabotage. And the fear they incite compels its targets to submit to their will with little or no resistance.

Mob bosses are great examples of those who operate with callousness. In this instance, the agent of sabotage may not always be the actor who executes the betrayal, theft or deceit; instead, they use their influence to convince another person to do their bidding. In such a case, the person who actually does the act and the actual target both find themselves compromised by the bully.

Because these agents of sabotage are often cruel, disloyal and insensitive, they usually quickly—and coldly—dispose of those they get to do their bidding once they have received all they need or expect from them.

The most effective agents of sabotage driven by callousness pride themselves on their ability to recruit and bend others to their will. They operate with a confidence that there will always be someone available to use for their next act of betrayal, deceit or theft. All they have to do is appeal to that person's desire to feel like they are apart of something meaningful. The bully's promise to use their influence to benefit the person who will do their bidding also goes a long way.

These agents of sabotage also think highly of their ability to fight. They are willing fighters. So, when they carry out the act of bullying themselves, or some other form of sabotage, they do so prepared to defend against any resistance or accountability. They relish fighting because they see it as a way to stoke additional fear and bring those who seek to defend or rescue their victims to their knees. The most egregious of these agents of sabotage sometimes plan, well in advance, to fight and undercut law enforcement and the justice system in the event they need to avoid them to flee owning up to their acts.

OVERREACHING AMBITION

Ambition is an insatiable drive that compels people to accomplish and perpetually conquer. Ambition is a thirst that cannot be quenched. There is not enough food one can feed ambition to satisfy its desire for more. In fact, one could argue that feeding it only increases its appetite. This cycle makes it easy for people to become blinded by ambition.

Blind ambition can be likened to taking the side mirrors off of a car. The driver becomes so consumed with the need to arrive at a certain destination that they ignore the other cars on the road. With blind ambition driving the car, they have a blatant disregard of the danger driving without side mirrors might have on others.

Those blinded or driven by ambition sometimes suffer from an over-indexed perception of themselves. They always proclaim to be on their way to greater and better and often exhibit megalomaniac or narcissistic behavior. They believe in getting it done—not for the sake of the team, but for themselves.

They are also rarely where their feet are. In other words, they are always conjuring up the next pursuit or conquest. They often underachieve in executing anything that truly lives up to their original vision, largely because their vision is not aligned with or grounded in reality. This, in effect, drives them to quickly move on to the next conquest.

Ambition is a strong force. Of the many adjectives used to describe ambition—desire, zeal, and determination—attributes like loyalty and honesty don't make the cut.

RESISTANCE TO ACCOUNTABILITY

Agents of sabotage who want to avoid accountability often start out by growing a disdain for authority. Their disdain is not necessarily about supervision, but more about a longing to control their environment to feed their need for predictability.

Supervisors, or those in authority, threaten this predictability because of their ability to assign expectations and accountability at a moment's notice. Those susceptible to using resistance to avoid accountability often view constructive criticism as personal judgment and want to avoid situations or work environments that demand visible performance or consequential work.

They want to operate below the radar while performing work that allows them to quietly make moves without drawing much attention.

When their management environments change to increase their exposure to accountability—either by the introduction of new management, new priorities, or newly assigned roles that impact the resistant person—they respond with defiance. When their defiance is pronounced, this will be expressed by wielding victimhood, pouting, sulking and making it difficult for managers to implement new measures, initiatives or priorities.

Another weapon includes making false accusations against others, including managers, to have them removed as to eliminate the threat of being assigned accountability.

When their weapons of defiance are less pronounced, these agents of sabotage shut down completely—becoming less available to management and visibly closed off to new responsibilities.

These defense mechanisms help them avoid ever having to perform, execute or be accountable. And your organization's growth is the biggest casualty for their selfish needs.

In effect, their resistance to accountability manifests itself as quitting. And as a leadership maxim goes, people who quit on themselves, will quit on you. It's only a matter of time.

THE DESIRE TO OPERATE BEHIND FALSE FRONTS

As an evolution of lying to yourself and others is the concocting of whole worlds that are grander than one's reality. These false worlds are then leveraged by these agents of sabotage for personal gain. Flattery is a common tool for these agents of sabotage. As a weapon, flattery attempts to distract unassuming victims of sabotage from the malice at hand— causing them to bring down their defenses by appealing to our need to feel valued.

These agents of sabotage are attractive. They curate their appearance and are charismatic operators. They lead lives that appear grander than their realities. Thus, they must work exceedingly hard to conceal the reality of their true lives, even if it means leveraging their false grandeur to appear more responsible and credible than they really are.

The problem that fantastic storytellers face is that the image of an outsized lifestyle and credibility that they project requires constant maintenance. As a result, their false lives will never be rooted in truth. There will be inconsistencies and gaps that must be filled with more lies and deceit to hold the fantasies together. They need to conceal their reality from those who invest credibility and responsibilities in them. One exposed inconsistency, and the house of cards will come tumbling.

These agents would rather sabotage others than be embarrassed and exposed.

— — —

Understanding what drives agents of sabotage is just as important as protecting yourself against them. Being able to see the early signs and warnings of these invisible acts is an advantage, but knowing what to do when you find the stars aligning around sabotage is just as important. Let's get into how to stop each Horseman in its tracks.

THE BRIEF

There are eight things that drive people to sabotage:

1. Unfulfilled personal needs
2. A desire to act out the lives of others
3. A penchant for lying
4. A desire to correct a perceived wrong
5. Callousness
6. Overreaching ambition
7. Resisting accountability
8. A desire to operate behind false fronts

PROTECTING
YOURSELF FROM THE
FOUR HORSEMEN
OF SABOTAGE

CHAPTER FOUR

THE FIRST STEPS TO ARMORING YOURSELF AGAINST SABOTAGE

A s a communications and organizational consultant, I've seen countless examples of the effects of sabotage on organizations and their leaders.

One example involved a church led by a devout, and in many respects, legendary community leader. His kind heart made him the perfect target for betrayal. For more than thirty years, he ran his church as a business that gave to the community, and benefitted the lives of those in his congregation—even giving money and supplies to families to allow them to build better homes, providing jobs to those who needed support, and even adopting abandoned and abused children, taking them into his home as his own.

As a result of his effectiveness, his fruits were plenty. The houses he helped build still stand today. Those he was generous to now give to others, and those he saved from abusive homes are now wealthy, prominent business leaders as adults.

Personally, I consider this pastor to be my spiritual mentor. In my opinion, he is the wisest man I know.

There is a saying that perhaps best describes the guile of an agent of sabotage. It says, "When the grass is cut, the snakes will show." This pastor's grass cutting became a necessity when his health declined, thus taking a toll on his strength, focus, and financial resources. The agents of sabotage in his life revealed themselves. While he laid in the hospital recovering from a surgery, one of the leading voices among the deacons at his church presented himself as the savior to what he called "the embattled church."

He emerged among the flock with tales of doom for the church due to the pastor's declining health, and he asked that they follow him to start another church.

This deacon refused his former pastor's phone calls as he laid in the hospital recovering, and allegedly redirected funds from the church to war chests to be used to fund his own church. He gave prominent members of the congregation leadership positions to entice them to leave and led an exodus to start another church around the corner.

Some of the families the elder pastor helped fled with the agent of sabotage. Those the pastor helped for years turned their backs on him to join the betraying leader's new vision. The betrayal robbed the pastor of growth for his congregation, but also denied him the enjoyment of the return on the investments he'd made for decades in the agent he trained and poured effort into.

But even more, the sabotage posed a direct affront to the pastor's livelihood. The church was an engine for income for his life, and a smaller congregation meant a new financial reality for the pastor.

When the leader chose to become an agent of sabotage, he defied his intended purpose of being a legacy to the pastor's vision for the church it had taken him more than thirty years to build.

In a conversation with the pastor months after the betrayal was revealed, I asked if he saw the betrayal coming.

He admitted that it had been revealed to him in a dream, thus giving him time to prepare, protect and salvage the core of what he'd created. As a result, his ministry continues today.

Unfortunately, not all betrayal can be revealed in a dream, but we can identify it in the same way we might approach discovering why something is broken.

When things break—or betray us—we generally do a few things. First, we diagnose the cause of the problem. We may do this ourselves or call in an expert.

Secondly, we find the root cause of the problem by analyzing the reasons for the dysfunction.

Lastly, we remove the part or parts and either repair them or replace them with new ones. (As a note, choosing to repair the part often leads—in time—to a reoccurrence of the dysfunction.)

As we approach analyzing things that betray us, we too must take care to analyze why people may be compelled to betray us. We must analyze the chief weakness in a person's life the way one would determine what caused something to break.

We must then determine the forces that influence agents of sabotage—considering if the person has remained in a function too long and thus has deteriorating focus and faith or if they have been impacted by outside influences. Then we must act decisively to remove them from our lives once they are known.

Taking these steps is effective once the betrayal happens, but imagine having the power to diagnose the potential for human betrayal before it actually strikes our life.

There are typically three identifiers to look for to discover betrayal before it strikes:

- the level of disenchantment a person has for your leadership
- someone's tendency toward disdain and defection
- outside influences on someone's life

DISENCHANTMENT WITH THE BUSINESS OR LEADERSHIP

There will be times when those you lead simply stop believing in your company's mission. They will also stop having faith in your ability to lead in ways that bring that mission to life. When this happens, the associate might be tempted to betray.

SUSCEPTIBILITY TO DEFECTION

Those in our organization work with intent. They invest their sweat and thought equity in hopes of receiving a return on that investment. They also pre-determine when they believe that return should come—be it a raise, promotion, etc. When this does not happen, or if they have been at an organization for a long time and have no more promotions to enjoy, they are poised to defect from your leadership.

NEGATIVE OUTSIDE INFLUENCES

Those you lead will have their own network of advisers and influencers. This is a great thing. It brings to bear mentors that can help strengthen those you manage. But when these outsiders instill bad habits and influence those you lead in adverse ways, your team members become vulnerable to being a vehicle for betrayal.

Assess these areas of your life and receive insights into what could be fueling betrayal within your orbit.

— — —

What makes betrayal difficult to discern is that it operates in duplicity and deception. Because we must be trained to identify these things, we often don't have the tools to see the act because it is cloaked in secrecy. That is, however, until it strikes.

Because we know how to diagnose broken parts, we have the tools to analyze one's potential for betrayal long before it happens, and thus prepare safeguards to protect our lives from their impact. Each horseman requires a different tool— let's open the toolbox.

THE BRIEF

We must analyze why people may be compelled to betray us, the same way we try to figure out what made something break.

There are three identifiers to look for to discover betrayal before it strikes:

1. The level of disenchantment a person has for your leadership
2. Someone's tendency toward disdain and defection
3. Outside influences on someone's life

THE FIRST HORSEMAN:
JEALOUSY

———

CHAPTER FIVE

WHEN AGENTS OF SABOTAGE WANT WHAT YOU HAVE

Jealousy is one of the most intoxicating motivations for sabotage. It is also the most misunderstood.

Jealousy is hatred or resentment that fuels a longing to possess what others have.

Unlike any of the other Four Horsemen of Sabotage, jealousy as a motivation has the highest ceiling for escalation. If unchecked, it can take on many forms—compelling those it consumes to obstruct, damage or destroy leaders both personally and professionally. These agents of sabotage attack a leader's ability to perform, and do so in an effort to undercut that leader's ability to enjoy continued success.

Some of the most recognizable tactics of agents of sabotage who are motivated by jealousy include marginalization, concealment, and credibility assassination.

When jealousy seeks to marginalize leaders, it is typically done by agents of sabotage who have earned the confidence of those they loathe. They use their perch as trusted advisors to dissuade their targets from pursuing noble and worthwhile efforts. These agents convince their targets that their abilities are insufficient, or encourage the leader to abandon their dreams of pursuing greater for themselves. In some of the most extreme cases, the agent of sabotage would then pursue the same opportunities and dreams they encouraged their targets to abandon.

When jealousy operates in concealment, the agent of sabotage hides and stows away contacts, resources and opportunities that could benefit the leaders they resent. By limiting their target's exposure to promising opportunities, they, in effect, limit the leader's ability to advance.

And lastly, when jealous agents assassinate their target's credibility, they do so through mockery or outright degradation of the leader's ideas and initiatives. In this case, they hope to conceal their attempt at assassinating their target's credibility under the guise of good humor—all in an effort to buy time to convince others to see their target as a leader who lacks credibility.

Jealousy is often misunderstood because it can take many forms, including covetousness and envy. However, in its simplest and most recognizable form, jealousy is a mere concept. We've all experienced this feeling before. Fortunately, many of us have the emotional tools to dispel jealousy before it can take root in our lives.

As a notion, jealousy has a familiar script. That script sounds like, "I wish that was happening to me." Or, "I wish I had what John Doe has."

At this stage in its development, the roots of jealousy are so weak that they can easily be removed from our lives without motivating any, or much, action.

While in college, I recall being jealous while preparing my campaign to become president of the student government association. One of my fiercest competitors was someone who had earned the support of influential and powerful student groups on campus. Past candidates for student government president who had earned the support of these groups won the election almost 100% of the time. I know that data point because I had studied it and failed in my attempts to win the support of these same influential student groups.

But I ran for president anyway. Even though I was considered an underdog, I campaigned enthusiastically.

During the hard-fought campaign, I repeatedly wondered what it would be like to have the support and momentum that my competitor had worked hard to earn. I stopped that jealous thought there. Realizing that my supporters believed in my candidacy just as much as anyone else helped me remain content with my fortunes and proud of the campaign I ran.

Not intending to bury the lede, I lost the election. But to this day, decades later, I still encounter alumni around town who remember my campaign and what it stood for.

If I allowed that jealous notion to take hold and fester, it could have easily escalated into something more dangerous: the form of jealousy fueled by covetousness.

Covetousness is a form of jealousy that's fueled by desire and yearning. This is more than a notion. It is spoken intent that, if left to its own devices can spur supporting action.

Covetousness has a voice. It speaks with resentment and reveals itself as a nudging that sounds like "Why is John Doe always the one who gets selected for..." or "Why does everyone believe Jane Doe is capable of delivering what is being asked for?"

This resentful jealousy can motivate those it consumes to start exploring the feasibility of marginalizing or undercutting the leaders they resent.

This feeling was a motivating factor for Tonya Harding, a once-famed figure skater who is now infamous for her role in attempting to destroy Nancy Kerrigan's championship figure skating career in 1994.

In the 1990s, Kerrigan was a famed and accomplished figure skater who had earned a reputation as America's darling. The media swooned over her every move, making her a fan favorite for most of the events in which she competed. And, like most once-in-a-generation athletes, she often delivered. Her acrobatic feats and the grace with which she skated made her easy to love. That is, unless you were Harding.

Harding could not be more different than Kerrigan. Where Kerrigan was graceful, Harding was rugged. Where Kerrigan was easy and charismatic, Harding was gritty. However, it was Harding's tough character that contributed to her success as a figure skater. A high school dropout, Harding was raised by an oft-underemployed father and a mother who mostly worked as a waitress. Her background was so humble that her mother would often sew Harding's skating costumes by hand because they lacked the money to purchase the expensive competition outfits.

Harding coveted Kerrigan's success, grace and ease. Her jealous resentment was often on full display in media interviews where she lamented her constant role as the underdog to Kerrigan.

Harding's jealousy eventually became so unbridled that she made the decision to participate in sabotaging Kerrigan's figure skating career in 1994. Harding's on-again-off-again husband, Jeff Gilooly hired men to take batons to Kerrigan's knees during a practice, thus ensuring that Harding had a clear path to join the U.S. Figure Skating Olympic Team. Harding later confessed to knowing her husband wanted to "take out" her competition, but she didn't try to stop him, essentially letting it happen. She was convicted with hindering the prosecution in the case, but didn't serve any time in jail.

Now, violence motivated by jealousy is a very uncommon occurrence in most management and leadership cultures. But the crux of the matter should not be missed: if jealousy is allowed to remain and fester in our midst, it can quickly compel agents of sabotage to try to take that which they covet from you.

In its most extreme state, jealousy takes the form of envy. Where jealousy begins as a thought that evolves into a yearning, envy is a menacing trigger that compels agents of sabotage to undertake sustained—and sometimes elaborate—efforts to take what they want from the leaders they despise. They go beyond undercutting a leader's efforts into stealing.

One of my friends and his wife fell victim to an agent of sabotage who was motivated by envy. He and his wife joined forces to start a new company, and turned to a trusted associate to lend her expertise as the company's chief executive. My friend and his wife compensated this associate with a 25% ownership share of the company, in addition to other benefits.

What my friend and his wife didn't know is that although they'd known their trusted associate for years, she had been secretly waiting on the opportunity to act on the jealousy she had concealed for nearly a decade.

Serving as CEO of the company founded by the leaders she privately resented was the perfect opportunity to use their fortunes to harm them, while simultaneously enriching herself and using their resources to build her own company.

In an elaborate scheme, the associate worked overtime to stealthily recruit new clients to my friend's company. However, when she sent them the contract, she did so under the name of her own company, an LLC she founded and owned outright. The names of the two companies were likely intentionally similar, as many of the clients were none the wiser. Neither were my friend and his wife.

While attending a conference, my friend happened to converse with a man who was familiar with his company's work. However, when describing the company, the man mentioned a name that wasn't the name of my friend's company, and spoke of his associate and CEO with accolades far grander than he'd heard before. By the end of the conversation, he discovered the ruse, and quickly assessed the damage. By that time, their CEO had already transferred more than three million dollars from his company to enrich herself and satisfy her envy.

— — —

Jealousy must not be allowed to exist in your management culture. It is a divisive and debilitating force. And as a motivation, it can also be contagious.

Whether agents of sabotage are motivated by thoughts of jealousy, or consumed by yearning and envy, there are steps you can take to protect yourself and your leadership pursuits from its attacks:

CONCEAL YOUR INTENTIONS AS A LEADER AND MANAGER

We all want to share our desires and pursuits with others. Leaders and managers see these moments as opportunities to inspire others to share in the work to make their pursuits a reality. However, because their intentions might be in process, the leaders present enough data and insights to give agents of sabotage the opportunity to take undermining action.

Instead of broadly sharing your intentions, empower a small group of leaders to help realize specific outcomes that progress your overall vision. While they may not know the entirety of your pursuits, this approach gives you a chance to hold those you empower accountable for delivering specific results that advance the pursuit.

CREATE OPPORTUNITIES FOR UNDERDOGS TO BECOME CHAMPIONS

As leaders, we often have responsibility for managing multiple personalities and are charged with placing each person in a position to win. As a result, managers need to assess the strengths and weaknesses in their team. Whenever possible, create platforms—whether they be at department meetings or during one-on-one sessions with team members—to champion and celebrate when one of your team members does something that's outside of their comfort zone. This may not eliminate the presence of jealousy in your management culture outright, but it will go a long way in ensuring that every team member feels that their contributions aid in lifting the entire ship.

CELEBRATE GRATEFULNESS

Jealousy festers in environments consumed with discontentment. When people are unhappy with themselves and their circumstances, they become tempted to take the circumstances of others as their own. Limit this by being a leader who outwardly models gratefulness.

When people gripe about limited departmental budgets, focus on the good that can be done with what you've been given. When members of your team become frustrated with missed promotions or other opportunities, you can use the moment to challenge them to embrace their current blessings, and to not become consumed with what could be at the expense of what they have at that moment.

As a closing note, leaders who are grateful become servant-leaders. Service to others, in my opinion, is the acme of leadership. Encouraging those you lead and influence to join you in helping those in need could have the net effect of shaping the way they view themselves, their fortunes and their circumstances. Shifting your management culture to one that promotes service will help eliminate an environment that breeds discontentment.

THE BRIEF

Jealousy is hatred or resentment that fuels a longing to possess what others have, and has the highest ceiling for escalation of any Horseman. There are three levels to jealousy:

Jealousy: The common feeling of wanting what someone else has. It can sound like, "I wish that was happening to me." Or, "I wish I had what John Doe has."

Covetousness: A form of resentful jealousy that's fueled by desire and yearning that if left unchecked, can spur supporting action. It can involve thoughts like, "Why does everyone believe Jane Doe is capable of delivering what is being asked for?" and actions that undercut someone's effectiveness.

Envy: A form of menacing jealousy that compels agents of sabotage to undertake sustained efforts to take what they want from the leaders they despise. This can include elaborate plans to steal from their target.

How to protect yourself from jealousy:

1. Conceal your intentions as a leader and manager
2. Create opportunities for underdogs to become champions
3. Celebrate gratefulness

THE SECOND HORSEMAN:
LYING

—————

CHAPTER SIX

WHEN AGENTS OF SABOTAGE LIE

Liars are everywhere. I personally believe that there is no such thing as a small lie. All of them are big in my eyes, because as a leader, I rely on sound information to make decisions and plans about the things I want to accomplish.

People lie for many reasons. Compulsive liars lie out of impulse and habit. Then there are the willing deceivers, who lie to purposefully achieve a certain end or to conceal true intent.

Deceivers have dogged leaders since the beginning of time. Driven by a profound need to conceal their untruths, deceivers are constantly in a battle with themselves to mask vulnerability, weakness or inadequacy.

To compensate for their weaknesses, they skillfully weave webs of untruths to give them a sense of control, help them assume authority, enable them to gain intermittent victories and dodge accountability.

Liars want to believe the lies they tell. The shame that they feel and conceal is often so intense that they hide behind their web of untruths in an effort to be embraced and accepted in accordance with their lie, if only for a time. Leaders will inevitably encounter deception along the journey to achieving success. The first thing to remember is that the liar's motivations are rarely about you—they're about their own fears. So don't take it personally.

Liars are frightened to death of following leaders who invite them along their journey to redefine industries and chart new methods and practices. The accountability that accompanies such an invitation will demand that they live in truth. Liars can't do this.

Instead of rejecting the invitation, liars often lie and wait for an opportunity to derail and sabotage the entire pursuit—dousing cold water on the best laid plans, or stalling activities to ensure slow to no progress.

In simplest terms, liars lie because it's effective. Liars get what they are after more times than not. Such a thing can be costly for a leader. Here's how to find and stop deceivers before they strike:

STAY ENGAGED

Unengaged leaders make perfect targets for manipulative liars because they provide openings for the liars to access and shape data and information related to projects or operations. When liars assume this role, the temptation to cook the details or mislead can often be too great, and they will often do so to ensure that things move at their pace or to conceal the personal inadequacies that consume their lives.

Liars often micromanage or dominate dialogue in an attempt to hide their true intentions. Take an interest in the work they do by constantly asking about their challenges and supporting their solutions. Also, follow up frequently to keep a pulse on progress and impact.

FACE THE LIAR HEAD-ON

The reason many liars benefit from the webs they weave is, in part, because we deal with liars poorly.

Our default approach is often avoidance. As professionals, we typically isolate those who lie, limiting interaction and engagement. It is unrealistic to believe that avoidance is sustainable when your leadership requires that you have command of large organizations, or when part of your responsibility is to inspire diverse teams of professionals to work toward desired results.

For leaders, truth is the most potent weapon against dishonesty. I personally use it often—calling out liars and their lies and leading in ways that demand that my team verify the information they submit. By confronting liars with truth, leaders put themselves in the best position to protect those they lead, and their efforts from sabotage.

A friend of mine experienced the effects of working at an organization that chose avoidance first-hand. While a middle manager at a bank, the aspiring investment banker was gaining the experience he needed to achieve his career goals. With a child at home, a pregnant wife, and a 2009 economic slump, my friend had little room for error as he worked and studied for his MBA at a local university.

One call from the human resources department threatened all of this. On that morning, he was asked if he knew an African-American associate we will call Jane Doe.

My friend, a white male, said he did not, and without a picture or physical description, he couldn't pinpoint the associate in question.

He was then told that he was going to be the subject of an internal investigation because Jane Doe had alleged that he had used racist slurs towards her. He was shocked.

For six months, he worked under extreme anxiety, not knowing if all he was building would be stained by the erroneous claim of racism.

Towards the end of the investigation, he learned the identity of the accuser. The lack of evidence of Jane Doe's claims suddenly became clear as he realized that the accuser was someone he'd never engaged with. The bank was rather large and their departments didn't overlap.

While at night school studying, he and a colleague discussed the stress of those six months. When he shared the nature of the accusation against him, her jaw dropped in amazement. She'd heard similar stories about this Jane Doe three other times—all accusing a different white male at the company of similar racist acts.

It turned out that the accuser was serially concocting lies about being victimized by racism because the company met each claim with paid time off work.

The accuser was on a roll. Her lies threatened to ruin her targets, but earned her nearly a year and a half of paid vacation.

Shame on the company's leadership for not protecting their employees once it was discovered that the lies were habitual.

LEARN AND VALUE THE ROLE OF EACH TEAM MEMBER

Just as a quarterback knows the route assignments of each wide receiver, leaders must also know their team's respective roles and responsibilities. This allows the leader to be in a position to literally keep things honest.

REWARD FACT AND TRUTH

Leaders work and plan best when given reliable facts and data. Reward honest contributions from your team. Create an environment where facts are valued by encouraging research. When untruths are detected, call them out—regardless of how small. Place a large spotlight on the untruth, and name it. Reward truth with the same vigor.

Applying these tools will help you build a leadership culture that repels dishonesty and compels honesty. As you saw with my friend who was nearly taken down by Jane Doe, a persistent culture of lies will only breed discord in your organization.

THE BRIEF

Liars lie to achieve a certain end or conceal their intent.

How to stop liars in your midst:

- Stay engaged
- Face the liar head-on
- Learn and value the role of each team member
- Reward fact and truth

CHAPTER SEVEN

WHEN AGENTS OF SABOTAGE STEAL

M ovies and television shows often depict theft as a high-stakes exercise that involves scaling tall buildings or forcibly breaking and entering someone's property.

Thanks to these movies and the real accounts of theft that may have impacted those close to us, we know how to respond: Call the authorities and ask that they open an investigation.

I've had to do this in my career as a chief executive. I am sure many of you have. As a leader, theft has a high possibility of striking. As a result, being prepared to respond to theft is usually high on the priority list of crisis management tools we often sharpen.

In my case, I had an employee steal a computer from the office. It was quite a brazen act. After hosting a meeting to end her employment at the company, she bolted out of the room, running up and down the hallway spewing profanity at anyone in earshot. She ended her rant at the office where her belongings were kept. Her erratic behavior caught the security escort who was supposed to guide her out of the building completely off-guard. Before we knew it, she had unplugged her company-issued computer and began walking out of the building with it.

I watched from afar as she threatened legal action on anyone who attempted to stop her.

My response was easy. I had a restraining order drawn, and filed criminal charges.

However, in reality, the acts of theft that confront us most often are a little less extreme, and therefore trickier to address. They amount to an avalanche of micro-aggressions that, if unaddressed and unnoticed, can sink what a leader aims to build.

These micro-acts of theft include secretly stowing away a company's database of clients, trade secrets and high value network rosters to be used later for personal gain. Another example would be soliciting clients away from a current employer and asking them to become clients of a private venture to be activated once the employee quits.

I'm not discounting that theft of money happens at the work-place—we've seen the multiple indictments of people who use company resources and credit cards for personal benefit. However, the micro-acts of theft detailed in this chapter are the building blocks that can lead to the earth shattering dis-coveries within our organizations.

One of my clients experienced this first-hand—let's call her Sue. While serving as the president and chief executive offi-cer of a large multimillion dollar not-for-profit organization, she found herself enduring great duress.

Many of Sue's partners began to accumulate arrearages by either refusing to pay their obligations or paying them late. Because her partners were so large, many of them Fortune 500 companies, the debt they held was massive. At one point the monies owed to her company reached more than one million dollars—a crippling amount of money for a nonprofit to have outstanding.

Employees worried. Furloughs were initiated. Belt tightening was in order. Sue was confident in her ability to manage her organization through these tough times.

However, one leader wasn't so convinced.

This employee—let's call him Andrew—was a leader within the organization. He had a large staff reporting to him, and a broad set of responsibilities. He also enjoyed great influence within the organization.

During the time of financial duress at the organization, Andrew bided his time by stealthily recruiting staff members to eventually resign and join him in starting another company. The company he was planning to start would do the same work as Sue's company and presumably would do that work for the same clients.

Andrew solicited current clients. He encouraged them to transition their contracts from his current employer to his private venture. He promised to sweeten the deal by providing lower prices.

Once he felt all was in place, Andrew resigned, seemingly out of the blue.

His departure seemed logical to Sue. The organization was enduring financial stress, and she just assumed that Andrew was getting out to protect himself. She was actually relieved by his resignation, as Andrew was a constant drag on employee morale.

About a month after Andrew's resignation, the true reason behind why he left the company became clear.

Sue received a phone call from a college president they'd worked with for years. The college president told her that they had been contacted by Andrew, soliciting them to join his company. The president investigated the matter and discovered that the solicitations dated back to when he was still employed at the nonprofit organization.

To make matters worse, not only was he asking for their business, Andrew also began using the methods from his former employer to solicit them to become his clients.

He had stolen, and stowed away secret methods from his former role, and was now peddling these valuable possessions to steal clients to start his own company.

In our careers, we hear of these kinds of acts often. We typically think nothing of them because people do it all the time—taking clients and databases with them as they move from agency to agency.

Leaders must not grow comfortable with these unethical actions. If they are allowed to persist, they could escalate into something that can't easily be undone.

When the nonprofit chief executive had a chance to confront the former employee-turned-rival, she asked him one question that he couldn't answer: Why didn't you call me and share your desire to work with those you were secretly soliciting away from me?

His response was cold: "I did what I felt I had to do."

He simply felt under-appreciated and unhappy while at the organization. He felt he had no choice but to steal.

Not all unhappy employees steal, but those who steal from their leaders are almost always unhappy—either with themselves or with the organization.

His subversion gives leaders a lesson for surviving and deterring theft within our leadership lives—in short, ensure that employee morale is high.

I believe people steal from those they've grown a callousness for. Such insensitivity develops over time. The Petri dish is often unhappiness. Although all employees can't be made happy, a leader can choose to strive to boost morale every day.

The chief executive in this story failed by not addressing the growing unhappiness of her employee sooner. He shouted for help with his defiance, and screamed that he was unhappy with his inflexibility. His leader didn't respond to the calls.

This chapter is not so much about surviving theft as it is about curtailing it from your leadership culture. Build a leadership culture that empowers, offers collaboration, provides ample opportunity for input—and most of all—one in which each associate cares about the other.

One legendary business leader put it best when he said, "If I can't help make you happy at my workplace, then it is my job to help you find another place to work."

There is a lot of truth in that statement.

THE BRIEF

Stealing can be brazen, like stealing an object or money. It can also be a collection of subtle micro-acts of theft that are harder to notice, such as stealing client lists or trade secrets for later use.

Ensure employee morale is high, as people steal when they've become unhappy.

THE THIRD HORSEMAN:
ARROGANCE

———

CHAPTER EIGHT

WHEN AGENTS OF SABOTAGE BULLY

L ike many of you, I have battled with a bully. My battle came while I was working to build a reputable company in an industry where the rate of failure is high. I touched on this story in the introduction, but it's worthwhile to revisit it in more detail here.

In 2012, my business was very successful. I was making a lot of money and enjoying every minute of it. My clients also enjoyed our services. Things were so good that my wife and I decided to do two things that would change our lives forever:

- We decided to expand our family and move to another home to support the addition.
- We also discussed my business strategy, one that entailed acquiring other companies as a way of continuing our growth.

A phone call from a friend promised to be the thing that could set everything in motion. My friend shared that an incredibly influential businessman in my hometown had convinced the owner of one of the oldest businesses in America to sell his company to me. He finished the call by saying that the deal was assured to make me millions of dollars. I was elated.

That phone call would result into one the most regrettable introductions of my life.

To protect the identity of the would-be seller, we will simply refer to him as Cain. Cain was a bully.

In the first year of my relationship with Cain, I allowed myself to be manipulated. Cain invited me to enter into a mentor/mentee relationship with him, falsely promising to make me rich and preparing me to acquire his company. He used that relationship, along with his far-reaching political influence, to strongly encourage me to take some bad business advice.

I agreed, in good faith, to merge my company's assets with his to form a joint venture and make contributions to the joint venture while performing due diligence on his business—all against advice of legal counsel. That manipulation cost me more than $15,000 each month until he sold me his business.

Cain enjoyed the fruits of this unbalanced relationship so much that he created one excuse after another to delay the selling of his business to me. In the interim, he saddled me with challenges to prove my mettle—challenges that really only sought to grow his business. An example of such a challenge included using me to retain and renew his expiring client contracts. He leveraged such challenges as conditions for selling me his company and making me millions of dollars. I met every challenge.

In the end, almost two years later, my attorneys discovered that Cain never used the investments I contributed to set up our joint venture. He used that money to enrich himself instead.

After discovering that I had been fleeced, I quickly moved to formally dissolve our relationship. I stopped making contributions to the joint venture that didn't exist. I empowered my attorneys to draw up formal separation documents. These actions were like punching the school bully in the face at high noon during lunch time. Unfortunately for me, my bully punched back.

He refused to sign the separation documents. He countered by threatening my employees with physical harm if I refused to give him more money. He threatened to harm my wife— literally promising to "kill her" by sending me to jail and making me a criminal. When those threats didn't compel me to give him more money, he took action. He called the police. Cain launched a criminal investigation and accused me of several white collar crimes—including fraud and theft.

It was a horrible time for me and my family. My wife and I had to delay our plans to move into a new home and have a baby. That money instead had to be used to pay legal fees and keep what remained of my business afloat.

Each day, I waited by the phone for a call from my defense attorney to learn if Cain's influence extended to the district attorney's office. He had the chief of police, the mayor and other political leaders indebted to him for one reason or another, so adding the district attorney to the list of his allies didn't seem like a stretch. Fortunately, his influence stopped there. If he did have influence with the district attorney's office, those false charges against me and his political clout could have resulted in jail time for me.

It didn't and I live to tell the story.

The total sum of the contributions I made to the joint venture that never was—including legal fees to protect myself during the separation—totaled nearly $700,000. It could have all been avoided.

Here are some lessons I learned to help you avoid the losses that come with mixing with people who use bullying to sabotage.

DON'T MIX WITH BULLIES

Generally speaking, bullies do not make great partners. By definition, bullying is a distinctive behavior of harming others.

According to research by *Psychology Today,* the act of bullying is persistent and durable because bullies usually get what they want at first. As a result, they want more of that thing, and strike out aggressively when they can no longer get it.

Bullies don't play fair and inherently search for weaknesses in those they come in contact with. As a business partner or a partner of any kind, their behavior will persist, and they will find ways to benefit and take more than the partnership allots. They will sabotage the partnership and its pursuits.

If they are in your organization, use your leadership to challenge and remove their aggressive behavior. If they are a client, request another representative to work with or move on. If the bully is anywhere within your leadership orbit, do not mix with them. Protect your leadership pursuits from involving them, and call their bullying out if they try to force themselves into your life and leadership. As a special note, these actions also apply when your bully is someone who supervises you. Avoid the relationship at all cost.

IF A BULLY STRIKES YOU, HIT BACK

Because bullying is a destructive act of aggression, it's a persistent act of sabotage. When bullies strike your leadership or those you manage, it is imperative you hit back. Psychologists point to the deliberate persistence of bullying as one of its distinctive traits, so standing down will not cause bullies to go away. Hire attorneys and surround yourself with allies, who can wield influence, or the law if needed, to send the message that the activity is not welcome within your life. Bullies must never be suffered.

WHEN BULLIES THREATEN YOU, BELIEVE THEM

In my experience, threats from my bully were not empty words. He used his threats to harm and steal from me. When you are threatened by a bully, take careful notes. Their threats detail all of their steps. Use what you learn to establish safety measures for those you lead, since they could be used as bait to get you to personally engage with their bullying. Lastly, find time to tell others in your high-valued networks and people the bully admires about the matter. Encourage them to use their resources to act on the bully and surround him or her before they can act.

WHEN BULLIES TRY TO DISTRACT YOU FROM YOUR LEADERSHIP PURPOSE, SHARPEN YOUR FOCUS

Such acts could include the bully refusing to leave your office until they get what they demand, threatening your employees or engaging in campaigns to harm your reputation. Before these actions are underway, plan ahead by supplying your staff with security measures for booking meetings for you and for screening office guests. Have talking points prepared for use in the event someone you do business with is on a reputation-damaging campaign. And lastly, hire an attorney—or activate the one you have on retainer—to manage these processes for you. An attorney's involvement will be well worth the money. As an investment, it keeps you from becoming distracted from leadership matters that truly matter.

WHEN BULLIES TAKE LEGAL ACTION, COUNTER THEM WITH LEGAL ACTION

When bullies take legal action, hit back. If it comes to this, be prepared. Because your attorney should already be engaged, then they should be on high alert for a few potential missteps that bullies might make. One of them is engaging your clients, or those you work with, in an effort to weaken that working relationship. This could actually be against the law, opening up the door for a lawsuit for tortious and willful interference with a contractual relationship. If your bully or his team comes to your office and refuses to leave, it opens up the opportunity for them to be removed by force and banned for harassment. Because I am not an attorney, lean on them for other strategies to ensure your presence is felt.

Bullies hate to be hit back. They loathe it. So hit back when you are confronted.

$- - -$

The only skill bullies possess is taking from others. And secretly, most bullies know they are not very capable when it comes to creating their own way.

To hamper any bully, the most powerful weapon you can use is to completely ignore the strength they attempt to project. The second most powerful weapon is resistance. Hit them where it hurts by refusing to give them what they want.

To many, this is easier said than done, especially considering that a bully's intimidation can feel imminent at the time of their leverage. However, choosing not to relent is equal to building a fence that guards the independence you need to be an effective leader.

As painful—and expensive—as my engagement was with a bully, the fact I'm most reluctant to admit was that I chose to engage. I chose to give him what he wanted. I chose to give him my partnership. In doing so, I also elected to sacrifice my autonomy as a leader.

Reclaiming my autonomy and restoring my independence cost me nearly $700,000. But in the end, I survived.

Let my survival give you the strength you need to resist your bully when they pound their chest.

Let my survival motivate you to hold fast to your independence and autonomy.

And finally, let my survival serve as a reminder that bullies can only appear as large as you make them.

So, make yourself a giant leader, and in turn, shrink every single bully that is in your midst.

THE BRIEF

Bullies sabotage through intimidation and force.

How to make bullies ineffective:

- Don't mix with them
- If a bully strikes you, hit back
- When bullies threaten you, believe them
- When bullies try to distract you from your leadership purpose, sharpen your focus
- When bullies take legal action, counter them with legal action

CHAPTER NINE

WHEN AGENTS OF SABOTAGE USE DEFIANCE TO SABOTAGE

D efiance is like a cancer to a leadership culture. It challenges a leader's ability to make consistent progress and always poses the risk of inspiring others who look to you for leadership to become defiant as well.

Leaders must take decisive and early action when faced with defiance.

At its core, defiance is a robust resistance to growth and advancement. Those who defy do so to slow down advancement or preserve their current status within a culture or organization.

Even though defiance has broad impact, the defiance is always solely about the needs of the defiant.

And yes, defiance is an act of sabotage.

By setting up a virtual tug-o-war within a leadership culture, defiance challenges all those the leader inspires to choose a side. When people defect and join the rebel by taking on similar tactics, the leader finds themselves—and their leadership pursuits—wounded.

Unaddressed defiance can lead to an organization where leaders appear to have lost total control. In these environments, leaders exist within an environment where employees believe they can exact a pound of flesh from the chief executive if he or she goes too far in their decision-making authority or stands in opposition to them in any way.

In my career as an organizational consultant, I've witnessed some extreme examples of defiance within organizations.

In one case, my client was the superintendent of a school system that was challenged with restoring excellence within the school district. The school system had an embattled brand and had been plagued by poor academic performance and student flight for decades.

Leader after leader had failed to successfully reset the organization's culture—all of them were terminated after about two years on the job.

The forces behind these leadership dismissals were school principals, who had used their influence with students as leverage to defy the vision of each superintendent leading the system. They worked together as a resistance coalition to stunt the organization's ability to improve its practices and excel performance.

They also worked doggedly to ensure the tenure of elected board members, and that administrators who were willing to hire their cronies and relatives operated with unchecked autonomy.

The resistance coalition would leap into action when the school system hired a leader who challenged this culture of defiance. They were usually effective—so much so that their actions often resulted in the unceremonious firing of the superintendent.

The defiance from the small coalition of principals had infected every operational rank within the organization—faculty bullied new teachers, staff ardently defied customer service training, and the board of directors protected principals opposed to achieving excellence for the organization.

It was truly the Wild West. The biggest losers were the students.

It can be difficult for a leader to regain management of a culture when it is taken by defiance. The superintendents I worked with, who were challenged with righting the culture and restoring academic excellence to the organization, learned this the hard way.

One superintendent, who I will call Bob, had a promising tenure. After taking aggressive steps to regain a culture of excellence, Bob turned his focus to removing the defiance within the organization. In doing so, he made the strategic decision to shuffle principal leadership to different schools, and bestow new levels of accountability for academic performance to disband the coalition of resistance.

Against professional counsel, Bob made one critical misstep: he telegraphed his intentions.

On cue, the leader of the defiant coalition, who I'll call Sally, reared her head—circling the wagons daring the superintendent to encroach on her previously unchecked authority. When he did, Sally struck. She met with students, sold them a story of personal victimization and assault on their school, and riled them up to speak out and defend her... I mean, defend themselves and their school.

The coalition supplied students with social media hashtags and news media contacts. They quickly planned and executed a school walk-out while the public watched. Their message to the superintendent was clear: "Leave our principal and school alone!"

Duped into believing they were fighting against a righteous threat, Sally successfully used the students as pawns to protect herself and her authority. Her message while the students protested was also clear: The students' unrest was evidence that Bob had lost control of the school system and was unfit to remain its superintendent.

Months later, the superintendent was terminated. Today, the principal who led the resistance has greater influence within the organization.

Defiance is an incredible study. It takes a variety of forms. Most common of these are aggression, avoidance, and passive aggression. When taking a closer look at the tactics used in each form, it becomes obvious that each is equally dangerous if unaddressed. Let's investigate each type of defiance and how to stop them in their tracks:

AGGRESSIVE DEFIANCE

Aggressive defiance is characterized as peacocking while an audience watches. Two examples include an operative sending emails to leaders that detail what one will not do, all while copying the entire world, or using noncommittal language to leader's requests while in a large group meeting.

Aggressive defiant people are typically not great team players. However, they are adept at using the team to meet their selfish ends.

Leaders must assign these people work to isolate them. They only know a language of derision, and will make several attempts to hack the leadership culture to bend the environment to their will. A clear recommendation is to remove them completely from the organization if you have the authority. If you don't have that authority, then refuse to provide them an audience for their defiance.

Schedule meetings with only you and another trusted adviser—never alone—and remove them from participation from large group meetings when possible.

When this is not possible, avoid giving them time during meetings—asking instead that they hold their questions until after the meeting and avoiding publicly assigning them responsibility.

AVOIDANT DEFIANCE

Defiance by avoidance requires cunning. Avoidant types are experts at evading responsibility and participation—and thus accountability—by conveniently being unavailable when needed. They often find themselves out of the office (on sick leave or vacation) during known busy seasons or when their time will be in high demand.

When they are in the office, they appoint themselves to the consummate role of office manager—delegating any responsibility to others as soon as it hits their desk. If leaders are not alert, they can confuse this tactic as management, when in reality it is classic avoidance. The litmus test for distinguishing the two is whether or not the defiant person is quick to blame others (or throw others under the proverbial bus) if something is not executed or if blame creeps close to their office.

Documentation is the weapon for defeating defiance by avoidance. Leaders must document every time they've had their requests for responsibilities shirked, or the number of times they've been unreliable for important contributions to the leader's pursuits.

Documentation helps to illustrate to the defiant person that you are aware of their track record, and thus prepared to take action to ensure that defiance does not infect others within the organization.

PASSIVE-AGGRESSIVE DEFIANCE

Passive-aggressive defiance is defined by incapability. Where aggressive defiance leverages things that one will not do, passive aggressive defiance exploits an inability to perform as their tool of resistance. This typically takes the form of being extremely busy all of the time, having overriding or more important responsibilities, or having other urgencies that they ask leaders to be sensitive to.

Not to be confused with avoidant types, these people typically don't use unavailability as their tool of resistance. They are present and available. However, with every request, they are adept at challenging leaders to consider their triaged set of priorities and responsibilities—thus making it difficult for the leader to ever involve the defiant. The defiant person secretly hopes the leader grows weary of considering the minutia of their workload that they stop giving them new responsibilities. This leaves the defiant person completely consumed and perpetually "busy" with only their priorities.

In my career, these acts of defiance are quite common. When possible, try to match them with strong and decisive managers—and always resist giving the defiant other people to manage. Failure to do so, could lead to you unintentionally giving them a platform for encouraging other associates to emulate their defiant behavior.

— — —

As a closing note, defiant people can have a change of heart. Through mentoring and training, some of them can actually decide to support the leader's vision and make valuable contributions to growth.

In cases where this does not transpire, they will continue to find ways to undercut the organization and your leadership for their own selfish preservation.

THE BRIEF

Defiance is a robust resistance to growth and advancement. Those who defy do so to slow down advancement or preserve their current status within a culture or organization.

The three kinds of defiance and how to stop them:

1. Aggressive defiance: This defiance is essentially peacocking in front of an audience. Isolate these people and try not to publicly assign them responsibilities.
2. Avoidant defiance: Avoidant types evade responsibility and participation—and thus accountability—by conveniently being unavailable when needed. Document these incidents so they're aware that you know their track record.
3. Passive-aggressive defiance: This typically takes the form of being extremely busy all of the time, having overriding or more important responsibilities, or having other urgencies that they ask leaders to be sensitive to. Match these people with decisive managers to hold them accountable.

CHAPTER TEN

WHEN AGENTS OF SABOTAGE HAVE OVERREACHING AMBITION

Ambition, as a character function, is not a recipe for success, but for dissatisfaction. People who have become overrun by ambition are rarely, if ever, satisfied. Those who have become consumed with ambition wake each day thinking of new ways to obtain conquests, accolades or self-aggrandizing roles—not to appease themselves—but to satisfy their ambition.

What many people who are over-ambitious fail to realize is that their ambition can never be satisfied—no matter how many accolades they feed it.

Bernie Madoff's life and legacy provide a glimpse into the behavior of over-reaching ambition.

Bernie Madoff is best known for stealing sixty-five billion dollars by orchestrating the world's largest Ponzi scheme. However, he stole much more than money. He stole the future from leaders of large corporations and foundations—and even the retirement funds of hardworking people around the world. Madoff then burned through the cash he stole by buying luxuries that made him appear more successful than he really was.

Madoff was known as a reserved operator. When in a room with some of the most elite, wealthy and powerful, he appeared understated. However, those in the loop knew him of his reputation as a financial wizard—a man who everyone clamored to invest their money.

Born in Queens, New York in 1938, his parents struggled financially. They endured the Great Depression. His father worked as a plumber until he eventually got into finance, and his mom was a dedicated housewife.

In the 1960s, young Madoff watched as his parents opened a financial company, only to have it shut down by the Securities and Exchange Commission (SEC) for improper disclosures. It is alleged that the business was placed in his mother's name because his father owed an enormous amount of federal taxes.

In retrospect, it appears these events made a deep impression on him. In an almost Shakespearean manner, the plight of his parents foreshadowed Madoff's life and legacy.

After graduating from Hofstra University, Madoff set out to achieve what had eluded his parents decades earlier. He opened his own financial company, Bernard L. Madoff Investment Securities, LLC. Because he was driven by ambition, realizing what his parents hadn't wasn't satisfying enough for him. He sought much more. So much so that Madoff used his company to steal billions of dollars from unwitting clients.

He made people believe it was a privilege to have him steal their money. He appeared successful. He held board positions that affirmed a narrative of accomplishment. And he had manufactured a reputation as a financial wizard, so people lined up to work with him.

Madoff netted approximately twenty billion dollars for himself from this scheme.

He swindled more than a thousand victims globally. The companies he swindled and the names of his clients read like a who's who in industry. They include the Royal Bank of Scotland, Grupo Santander, Royal Dutch Shell, and even former talk show host Larry King.

His list of victims is as diverse as it is long. It even includes teachers, small business owners and parents who entrusted him with their retirement funding.

He stole everything. Every penny. Every hope. His ambitions made it impossible for him to stop. It also made it impossible for him to care about the pain he caused. Madoff died in a federal prison while serving a150-year sentence.

But, the damage has been done. The lives of numerous people will never be the same. The humanitarian organizations he stole from have seen their philanthropy stunted. The futures of recently retired teachers and sanitation workers have forever been altered. All of this damage caused by Bernie's efforts to satisfy an unsatisfiable ambition.

Although our encounters with over-ambitious people will rarely be this extreme, we must make it a priority to not allow the ambitions of others to impede the things we are pursuing.

The more successful we are as executives, business owners and influencers, the more we will find ourselves surrounded by people who self-identify as ambitious. These same people will pitch themselves as a resource to you. They will seek to provide you with goods and services. They will attempt to give you advisory counsel and consultancy.

Buyers beware.

As with the case of Bernie Madoff, those who are consumed with ambition have their own priorities to address, and in most cases, see you solely as a vehicle for addressing these personal priorities. Any partnership that begins this way is fertile ground for sabotage.

Here's how to stop this kind of overreaching ambition from infecting your organization and impeding your leadership:

ENGAGE IN THE PROCESS OF RELATIONSHIP BUILDING

There comes a point in the lives of all leaders when we just need to get things done. At times we just need able bodies, brilliant minds, proficient managers or skilled consultants. And we need these tacticians yesterday. The pace of business and leadership can be fast. When leaders get swept up by the speed of business transactions, they can be lulled into dismissing the value of engaging in the slow process of building relationships.

Although not foolproof, building relationships is vital to reducing your exposure to agents of sabotage who are over-ambitious. Their tendencies, habits, consistencies and weaknesses are all attributes that reveal themselves over time. So, build meaningful relationships with people before you entrust them with large responsibilities.

TRUST, BUT VERIFY

People who make it into the small networks of highly effective leaders have typically earned their seat at the table through hard work. Their reputations precede them and other leaders often have only glowing things to say about their experiences working with them. When seeking recommendations for skilled professionals, asking those in your network is a strong start. But, more work is needed. Trust their references, but verify them by treading slowly. If you are eager to work with the professional in question, give them small responsibilities on the outset, thus creating opportunities for them to earn your trust with solid performance over time.

HIRE PROFESSIONALS WHO POSSESS THE ATTITUDE OF A SERVANT

In a world that often confuses ambition with hard work, it can be difficult to distinguish those who genuinely have a powerful work ethic from those constantly in search for their next selfish conquest. To help you make the distinction, it is important that we be very intentional about working with—and building relationships with—professionals who possess the attitude of a servant. Whether they be consultants, new employees or vendors, those who possess the attitude of a servant will always think of ways to put you, and your priorities, first.

When providing you with a service, they will very rarely think of themselves. They will also possess the confidence needed to make it easy for them to be a team player who is willing to work in every capacity of their expertise, i.e., if they own the delivery company, don't be surprised to see them making the delivery themselves if that's what it takes to meet your expectations.

Before you hire your next service provider be intentional about distinguishing those who are selfless operators from those who are driven by ambition. To do this, ask the prospective service provider to:

- Talk about the last time they failed to meet the expectations of one of their clients, and what they did to make it right
- Share the last time they faced an ethical dilemma, and what they did to overcome it
- Explain their most valuable client or business relationship and why they are so valuable.Those who are consumed with ambition will share only the things about the relationship that benefit them.

– – –

Achieving success requires that leaders work with other people. Encountering professionals who seek to sabotage us is an inevitable part of the journey towards achieving greatness. When hiring new professionals, appointing vendors or installing consultants, leaders must be prepared to embrace all of the risks that come with working with other people; we should do so with the same vigor that we embrace the challenges that come with each of our leadership pursuits.

Building relationships with the multitude of experts and professionals in our networks makes leadership rich. Embrace this adventure as you endeavor to carve out a special place for professionals who possess a servant's attitude.

As you scale the mountain of leadership, make these insights a permanent part of your toolkit.

THE BRIEF

Overreaching ambition can never be satisfied and will often run over others to achieve their goals.

How to stop overreaching ambition from effecting your leadership:

1. Engage in the process of relationship building
2. Trust, but verify
3. Hire professionals who possess the attitude of a servant

THE FOURTH HORSEMEN:
SEDUCTION

CHAPTER ELEVEN

WHEN AGENTS OF SABOTAGE OPERATE BEHIND FALSE FRONTS

In organizations with large and complicated organizational structure, leaders within them typically rely on others for reliable data and information. Some exploit this in their attempts to sabotage.

The associates they rely on have earned the trust and confidence of third-party influencers outside the company, and use these relationships to gain intelligence that can be shared with their superiors if necessary.

These associates fashion themselves as people in the know—and usually they are. Their chief currency is information, and they trade it like baseball cards for influence.

They relish in their role as gatekeepers of information. The most adept of these collectors of information operate behind the title of trusted adviser to the leaders who turn to them.

The roles of gatekeeper and trusted adviser create opportunities for these associates to betray those who turn to them for information or rely on them for their confidence.

When they betray, they do so in two ways. When they betray the leaders within their organization who rely on them, they do so by hiding behind intelligence they don't really have, or data that's been manipulated to meet their own selfish objectives.

When the betrayal impacts leaders outside of the agent's place of employment, they build false fronts as friend or confidant to those who give them access to information. The reality is that they are neither friend or confidant. Rather, they use the titles to mine data and information for the sole purpose of furthering their selfish causes.

In both instances, the person operates behind the false fronts.

One of my companies experienced the impact an associate operating behind false fronts can have on an effort to do something transformative when we wanted to help an organization establish high quality schools in low-income neighborhoods.

As background, my company has a long track record in education—serving as a consultant to Ivy League institutions and K-12 schools for more than seventeen years. In my mind and the minds of others, our selection as the agency of record was a no brainer. That was until the agent of sabotage decided to strike.

The agent in this instance was someone I perceived as a close associate—let's call him Dave. He was short of a friend, but someone I'd formed a friendly relationship with throughout the years of my professional life. He had assumed the role within his organization as a resource on matters of community engagement, and was asked often about such matters by executive leaders within.

Once we expressed our interest in being hired, we were shocked to learn that Dave was opposed to hiring us.

Working overtime, he erroneously attempted to connect my company to failed political leaders, and tried to cast me personally as someone not to be trusted. All the while, he posed to me as someone who was supportive of my work and the work of my company.

It was all very disappointing. Not just for me, but for the lives of countless families who could be served by the work we were to do.

In the end, our experience won the day. We were hired and would march aggressively to do the kind of work that exceeded expectations.

Surviving this attempt hinged on our ability to perform two things, which if used when faced with such betrayal, could prove effective.

The first thing we did was continue to deliver high-quality work products. From the initial proposal, to the analysis of our needs assessment, to the appearance and presentation of company associates, everything about my leadership exuded inscrutable professionalism.

The second thing I did was create separation between myself and Dave on a professional level. I did this by simply empowering others in my company to pitch this new client. If someone wants to discredit my leadership, fine, but it's difficult to also discredit the leadership of unknown employees within my company. This tactic can be referred to as moving the target.

It worked effectively. They had grown to trust those from within my company empowered to usher forth the results without bias. When some of the executive leaders convened to make their final decision about our company, one of the deciding factors was that although there are questions raised about my personal ability to offer leadership (information planted by Dave), it was clear that I would not be personally performing the work.

In executing the second aforementioned tactic, I enjoyed the net effect it had of elevating my personal leadership brand by showing an ability to astutely tap and train others to perform at a high level.

To control the impact from both of these tactics, all of my interactions with the company, moving forward, would be directly with chief, senior and board leadership within the organization. All engagement with the agent of sabotage would be designated to people within my company.

When dealing with associates who operate behind false fronts, the most difficult thing to achieve is identifying them as the agent of sabotage. This is so because they are operating behind a front. Although not foolproof, there are always red flags to note when dwindling down your list of would be culprits:

THEY ALWAYS ASK TOO MANY QUESTIONS ABOUT THINGS OUTSIDE OF THEIR OFFICIAL SET OF RESPONSIBILITIES

These agents must leave their base of formal responsibility in order to gain their currency: information from outside sources. In doing so, they often appear way more concerned and consumed with things outside of their formal scope of responsibilities. This is because they are trolling for data and information to trade to their leaders for more influence and promotion.

For example, such associates who work for a corporation (outside of governmental affairs) may always find themselves researching and befriending politicians to learn about matters that could be of value to leaders within their organization.

The promise to the politician (or whomever the giver of the information is) is always the same: I will use my influence from within the organization to look out for you if you are ever in need. This rarely happens because the person often, in reality, lacks the authority to make good on the promise. This promise is just another false front.

THEY WITHHOLD ACCESS TO INFORMATION CONCERNING MATTERS CONNECTED TO THEIR FORMAL RESPONSIBILITIES

Sometimes these agents of sabotage blur their lines of professional responsibility—misinterpreting data and information they've gained about matters outside of their formal roles and responsibilities with those directly tied to it. This misstep shows itself as those within your ranks who occasionally inadvertently refuse their leader, manager or supervisor access to data and information related to their formal job. Instead the associate asks that they be involved and consulted before any decisions are made about the data in their possessions.

This protectionism may be reversed later by the associate. But the presence of such actions reveals a penchant for operating in ways that are less than transparent.

THEY ALWAYS HAVE "A FRIEND" OR "RELATIVE" THEY ARE EAGER TO RECOMMEND FOR NEEDED WORK

Be mindful and cautious of those within your ranks who always have someone to volunteer for assignments, employment or responsibilities. They do so to cash in on promises they've made in exchange for intelligence from others or to position satellites who could undermine leadership at their command.

The need for reciprocity that's created from those who operate behind false fronts creates an environment where allegiances can easily shift away from the leader, in favor of those dealing behind the curtain.

The latter is the pretext for the creation of power vacuums and coups that overtake organizations and their leaders.

The steps to attack this kind of agent of sabotage are simple. First, when you discover someone dealing behind false fronts, always limit your exposure to them. Create a leadership path that travels above or around these operatives of sabotage, and deny them access to any data or information you don't want traded for their promotion.

And lastly, because you can't stop them from operating in the shadows, always lead impeccably and with honor to ensure they have a good show when they are watching you do your work.

THE BRIEF

Agents of sabotage who operate behind false fronts pose as friends or confidants to those who give them access to information. However, they only do this to mine data and information for the sole purpose of furthering their selfish causes.

Signs that someone is operating behind false fronts:

1. They always ask too many questions about things outside of their official set of responsibilities
2. They withhold access to information concerning matters connected to their formal responsibilities
3. They always have "a friend" or "relative" they are eager to recommend for needed work

When you discover someone is operating behind false fronts, limit your exposure to them and lead with integrity and honor.

REDUCING SABOTAGE FROM **YOUR LIFE AND LEADERSHIP**

CHAPTER TWELVE

BUILDING A LEADERSHIP CULTURE THAT REPELS SABOTAGE

⸺

Culture is like water to a fish. Whether that water is fresh, clean, salty, or polluted—figuratively speaking—depends upon the life and values of the culture's leader.

Every leader, intentionally or not, establishes culture by anchoring and sustaining a range of social norms and behaviors. It happens when they arrive to the office, make decisions about how to approach projects, manage finances and manage others. Every act and decision the leader makes helps to inform the culture.

When a leader is hired or assumes a role, everyone is watching. They look to see if the leader arrives to work on time, takes notes in meetings and respects the input of others.

Because people are hardwired for self-preservation, two things will always take place when a leader establishes a culture: those who look to the leader will either embrace and adopt the leader's values and character, or they will reject it and ultimately be pushed out of the leader's orbit. The latter is where I want to spend most of the time exploring the cultures we build.

It is the insights of those who leave or reject our values and character that tell us the most about ourselves. For example, if hardworking, honest and dedicated employees just keep leaving your leadership orbit, it's likely because you are not personally hardworking, honest and dedicated. The opposite is also true.

There are two leadership principles that anchor the alignment of those we lead with our character and value systems. They are the laws of attraction and replication.

The law of attraction speaks to the eagerness of those we lead to find commonalities that bond them to a leader and their culture. Simply stated, we attract the company of those who see common bonds with us.

While providing management consultancy to a president of a prominent university, I spent quite a bit of time with the leader (who I'll call Daisy) to understand her values, vision and character. The picture was rosy. Everything aligned perfectly. Except one thing was a bit off-kilter to me: the campus

Daisy was leading was being rocked by internal sabotage at every level.

Before I left one of our early sessions together, I told her that I appreciated her generosity and candor with me, then thanked her for opening up her campus to allow me to discover opportunities to reduce the infighting and backstabbing. When I left, I cautioned her that I would truly get to know her by getting to know the people she led.

She appeared worried by the statement.

After meeting her leadership team—staff leaders, faculty and student leaders—one thing was clear: they all existed within a culture of dishonesty. The truth was either weaponized for a benefit, or hidden to betray and deceive other unwitting colleagues.

It didn't take long for me to see the gap between what the president had shown me earlier, and the campus I experienced: the president led with a dishonest character.

Her dishonest dealings spread out and anchored the culture she had established and nurtured on her campus.

The law of attraction speaks to the attraction of ideals, more so than the recruitment of people. Every culture is known by its pace, rhythm and social behavior. If the leader is frenetic, the culture will be as well. If people are kind, then the leader too is likely a genuinely kind person. As a result, the ideals of sloth-fulness and unkindness will not persist within the culture.

The law of replication is another management philosophy that speaks to the alignment of the culture we establish. The law of replication states that those you lead will always do what you do before they do what you say.

The decisions you make as a leader signal what's permissible and what's not. If the leader allows the constant missing of deadlines, then others will believe that it's okay to do the same. If the leader berates employees in public, then others will believe this is acceptable behavior.

The law of replication even extends to matters that the leader doesn't believe others will see. This was the case for one CEO who accepted a job that required they live within a certain city. For very personal reasons, the leader, after receiving the job, decided to purchase a home outside of the city stip-ulated in the contract. The neighborhood the leader chose likely had larger homes and safer streets, but living inside of the designated city was part of an agreement she made upon accepting the job.

In an attempt at a sleight of hand, the leader leased a small apartment within the city stated in the contract once it became known that she was likely in breach of her contract. The leader never stayed, nor intended, to occupy the prop-erty she leased.

The leader established culture with this decision. Her actions unintentionally communicated to employees that it is okay to not honor your commitments and that one's personal desires should outweigh contractual obligations.

The decisions of the leader effectively created a culture that many came to know as inconsistent and unreliable.

To establish a culture opposite of this, leaders must live a life that's both consistent and reliable. Conversely, if a leader finds their immediate culture as one defined by laziness and ineffectiveness, finding the source only requires that the leader first look within.

These laws provide us keys to building a culture that repels sabotage, therefore protecting those you lead from it as well. If the ideals that stick within our organizations are set by the leader and people do as the leader does, then the first step to building a sabotage-free culture begins with you taking an assessment of your own character.

Character is the most important tool a leader can nurture, develop and invest in. Leading with great character sets a tone that those with poor character—like agents of sabotage—are unwelcome. It is also the most effective weapon against sabotage.

Character encompasses a leader's distinct temperament and integrity. Temperament speaks to a leader's management of patience and persistence along their journey of success.

Integrity is the strength of a leader's commitment to doing things the right way.

If a leader lacks in one of these areas, they could easily find themselves vulnerable to cutting corners or undertaking questionable tactics to meet an end. An example of this can be seen when genuine need meets opportunity. If the leader has weak patience and poor integrity, as soon as they are faced with a need—financial or otherwise—and an opportunity to quickly fill that need, the leader could be vulnerable to temptation.

Having good character causes leaders to do what they say they will do, and to do it the right way. When your culture is influenced by good character, then the forces that drive sabotage will find little ground.

But what do you do if you inherit a culture that's incongruent with your good character? In these cases, leaders must depend on another tool: Courage to be yourself.

Having the courage to let your light shine, to own your values and do what's right when it's not popular can have a powerful influence on the culture you exist in. The need for courage is high, because in cultures that are incongruent with your values, your very presence is a challenge to the status quo.

As a very young student affairs worker at a university, I was confronted with a student matter that I believed warranted expulsion. The university disagreed, and when the matter captured the attention of the national media, I was faced with a moment that tested my integrity. While preparing to be interviewed on the television network BET, lawyers rushed to tell me that I should not say publicly that the students should be expelled and that I should stick close to the university's commitment to investigate and suspend the students instead.

Joined by powerful board of trustees and with the nation watching, it didn't take long for respected journalist Ed Gordon to ask me the question concerning expulsion. Without blinking, I stood by my belief in stating that the students should be expelled. Everyone on the set was stunned and scrambled to salvage the message.

The next day, I was summoned by the university's president. Preparing to be admonished, I entered his office, ready to take my medicine—even termination from my on-campus job. The president slowly recounted the national media interview and the ire of those who saw my performance. He said that many had thought I was grandstanding and showed my youth when it mattered most.

I asked him what he believed. After a long pause, he declared that expulsion was indeed the right thing to do to the students in question. Following my lead, the university took measures to expel the students, and thus set in place a national model for confronting such student discipline matters.

They got there because of the courage I exhibited for doing what's right.

Regardless your position within an organization, when you operate with courage and character you instantly become a leader that others will look to, respect and grow to admire. You also become an influencer who—even if in a small way— can create opportunities to encourage behavior that repels sabotage.

THE BRIEF

Culture is a phenomenon that establishes, anchors and sustains a range of norms and behaviors in an organization. Culture is always set, augmented or affirmed by leadership.

Two outcomes of strong leadership cultures:

1. Those who look to the leader for cultural cues will either embrace the values and character of the leader, or
2. They will reject the leader's values and ultimately be pushed out.

Foundational laws for establishing a leadership culture:

- **Law of Attraction**—This law speaks to the eagerness of those we lead to find commonalities that bond them to a leader.
- **Law of Replication**—A management philosophy that states that those you lead will always do as the leader does before they do what the leader says.

Use these laws to build sabotage-proof leadership cultures by:

- Taking an assessment of your character as a leader
- Having the courage to be yourself when you inherit a poor culture. Your value system will, in time, impact the culture.

CHAPTER THIRTEEN

THREE ACTIONS FOR LIMITING YOUR EXPOSURE TO SABOTAGE

F amous musicians, actors and other celebrities attract large circles of "friends" into their entourage. Many of the people are looking for opportunities to make money, while others just want to leverage the fact that they are in the company of the famed.

Because the size of entourages balloon quickly, managing the access these people can have to the star can be an insurmountable task. As a result, these stars are inevitably exposed to risk. People in their entourage, be it a pretty girl or guy or manager, will usually ensnare the celebrity in schemes that result in millions in lost money or opportunity. The list of names of stars who have fallen prey to such sabotage is lengthy, including Sting, Rihanna and Billy Joel, to name a few.

As onlookers, we often ask ourselves how these stars could be so naive. Instead, what we really should be asking ourselves is if we are vulnerable to the risk of exposure to sabotage in our lives.

As a corporate executive, entrepreneur, or leader in general, you may not have multiple endorsement deals and a large entourage to manage. But what you do have is a long list of responsibilities and expectations to meet, as well as multiple divisions to manage and large numbers of direct reports to supervise. In a way, your risk to exposure to sabotage is no different than any star managing multiple deals at once.

There are three actions every leader should undertake to reduce their exposure to sabotage: Develop a power circle, slow down to speed up, and implement with clarity.

ACTION ONE: DEVELOP A POWER CIRCLE

If you follow the scams that derail famous people, they are usually orchestrated by managers, mom-managers, accountants or financial advisers. This is so common because many stars believe that having a small circle of service providers is synonymous with having a small circle of trusted advisers.

The difference between circle of trusted advisers and band of service providers is stark. The service providers are there for a fee and they provide a service that's guided by a contract. They would not be there if the contract or the fees didn't dictate their presence.

On the other hand, developing a small circle of advisers should provide for people who—although they may be paid—would be there for you regardless if the contracts ended or your influence dimmed.

When curated, your small band of advisers should become your power circle. A power circle can be defined as a group of advisers and confidants whose individual personal successes, knowledge and experiences can bring something to the table. They can be called upon to share their experiences as you wade through tough decisions and other matters.

Sometimes you may team up with people from your power circle to do something transformative, but partnering with them is not an expectation nor a necessity for their presence. The reason this circle is called a power circle and not an inner circle is because they voluntarily add power to your leadership and life—and you to theirs.

Having a power circle helps to insulate you from exposure to sabotage by providing you with a set of unbiased, independent ears and eyes. They believe in you and will share unvarnished perceptions about the things that could hinder your greatness. You can take it or leave it. But having a little sight in your blinders is always an advantage to leaders.

ACTION TWO: SLOW DOWN TO SPEED UP

Multitasking is a myth. Research from the American Psychological Association actually shows that it has the net effect of making you inefficient. It also can cause you to become overwhelmed and inconsistent. These are not characteristics typically associated with effective leaders.

Being a leader is as much about cultivating an ability to say no as it is about worrying about how much you can accomplish. Highly effective leaders strategically pick and choose where they spend their time and invest their treasure. When they make their decisions, they dive deeply and work richly in the few things that align with their priorities.

The act of limiting the things we undertake actually frees up leaders to produce more high quality, meaningful results. Working this way is all about working for impact.

The wisdom we commonly receive from others is that to accomplish more, we must do more. This couldn't be more inaccurate.

The great doers of our time have actually turned this idea on its head. They have achieved greatness by actually doing less.

Take Steve Jobs, whose story I discussed in the introduction. He was obsessed with developing a computer small enough to fit into the palm of your hand. Through his diligence, we now have the iPhone. By committing his leadership to this singular area of focus, he also helped make traditional computers smaller and more powerful. These accomplishments are a by-product of his focus and insistent commitment to learning all about what it takes to put the computer in your pocket.

Thomas Edison is another achiever who focused his efforts deeply and richly. He revolutionized modern society by developing ways to help us become better communicators. His narrow focus on this area drove him to develop the light bulb, the phonograph and the first motion picture camera— each transforming the way we share content with the masses.

In a practical sense, basketball players live by this principle. They believe that in order to become a well-rounded player, it is smart to spend the off-season diving deeply into improving one area of their game. Over time, all areas of their game will become stronger.

By limiting the things we devote our time to, we actually benefit from better clarity. The things that are important in our lives begin to come into sharper focus. Also, our personal networks become more tailored, aligning directly with the few priorities we choose to dedicate our leadership to. This alone will weed out would-be agents of sabotage.

Strategically and intentionally picking the areas we dedicate our leadership to reduces the forces of opportunism in our lives that agents of sabotage often use to set us up for betrayal, theft and deceit. Slowing down to speed up and doing less to achieve more positions you to have more control and leverage over your journey to having great impact.

ACTION THREE: IMPLEMENT WITH CLARITY AND ACCOUNTABILITY

For effective leaders, getting it done is not enough. They also care about how things get done.

Leaders who are thoughtful in execution enjoy great reputations, and their brands reflect positively on those associated with their endeavors.

An old mentor of mine, one with grey hair and a booming voice, once said that every leader must become skilled at setting traps and checking them constantly. In other words, establish a process for constantly receiving updates from those you manage to ensure their activities can be assessed and their progress evaluated.

Recognizing that it is probably not prudent to call these traps, I define this process of assessment as implementing accountability milestones.

Consistently checking with your circle of services providers and those you manage creates a mechanism for avoiding the development of accountability vacuums. Accountability vacuums are voids within your operation that lead managers and providers to believe that they will not be held account-able for their activity—or lack thereof.

Sabotage breeds in cultures with lackluster accountability.

There are a variety of ways to set accountability milestones in place. One of the more popular methods consist of weekly group meetings that allow those you manage to present their activity, and detail next steps. To make these meetings effec-tive in deterring sabotage, provide an open floor for others in the room to question the presenter's accounts and foster a clear tone of accountability and respect.

Another, oft-used method for creating accountability mile-stones is through one-on-one meetings. These meetings provide leader-to-leader discussions and allow for intimate discussions about the challenges, barriers and accomplish-ments of those you manage. These meetings should be treated as opportunities for thorough examinations of how respon-sible your team is being with the resources and instructions you've provided.

You'll know when things simply don't add up, or when someone is acting in a manner that's less than transparent. Providing yourself an opportunity to discern these moments is half the battle to building a leadership culture that repels sabotage.

Establishing methods for managing accountability is all about clarity. When empowering others to share in the execution of your priorities, it is important to never lose sight of your true aims or allow your mission to become clouded by the priorities or misdeeds of others. Keep your eyes on the ball. There is no greater and more effective way to execute.

– – –

When done in concert, these three steps will insulate your life and leadership from unassuming attacks from agents of sabotage. While there does not exist a way to completely remove the threat of sabotage from your orbit, reducing your exposure to it will make you sharper, more focused and alert, and thus more prepared to confront the challenges of sabotage as soon as they appear.

THE BRIEF

The three actions every effective leader should consider to reduce their exposure to sabotage:

Action one: develop a power circle

Those in your power circle should not be service providers. They are trusted advisers who can give objective advice, and would be by your side without your leadership mantle or large influence.

Action two: slow down to speed up

The great achievers in our society didn't get there by doing more to achieve more; they actually focused their attention on gaining mastery in a few things. Strategically and intentionally picking the areas we dedicate our leadership to reduces opportunities agents of sabotage often use to set us up.

Action three: implement with clarity

Leaders reduce their exposure to sabotage when they care about more than simply getting things done; they also care about how those things get done. Implement milestones to keep everyone accountable.

·

WHEN LEADERS
SABOTAGE
THEMSELVES

CHAPTER FOURTEEN

SOMETIMES THE MOST EFFECTIVE SABOTAGE COMES FROM WITHIN

U p until this point in the book, our study of sabotage has focused on avoiding and overcoming the methods and behaviors of people who betray, deceive and steal from us.

To be comprehensive, it is also important to acknowledge an important truth: We often betray, deceive and steal from ourselves.

Just as there are forces that power sabotage from others, there are also forces within each of us that constantly cause us to sabotage ourselves. Not all sabotage is external. The most effective betrayal can come from the person staring back at you in the mirror. The craftiest thief has our hands. The most elusive deception operates from within.

There are forces within us that, when ignored and unaccounted for, barricade us into lives of mediocrity, or worse, poverty. These forces range from self-doubt to low self-confidence. We will examine many of these forces in the following chapters. Regardless of what the forces are called, they each have the same mission: to stop us from living our very best lives.

As leaders, it is important that we see ourselves as the physical embodiment of the pursuits, dreams and the ideals we want to set in place for others. In doing so, we must also see ourselves as fair representatives for living our best lives, operating with integrity, and working with discipline to be intentional leaders. Above all, we must strive to live everyday with sound character. If we expect the organizations we lead to have each of these ingredients in order to be successful, then our lives must demand the same as a precursor to our personal success.

If sabotage tries to upend these ingredients to destroy the success of our organizations, then we must also come to grips that sabotage from within will do the same to our lives.

This section of the book focuses on fortifying your mind and emotions against the lies you tell yourself concerning what's possible and not possible in your life. These lies want to distract you from taking action that could lead to greater. These forces work daily, from within us, to make us believe we are not winners.

Winning—whether in life or business—is one of the most becoming characteristics of highly effective leaders. In fact, leadership is as much about living your best life as it is about any tactical pursuit.

However, there is not a lot of winning going on in the world.

Most people die without realizing their life's dreams. Personally, I am willing to bet that many of you reading this book are living a life somewhere short of your dreams. We all dream of having and achieving more, and desire greater for our lives. But, somewhere along the way we grew content with the lives we currently have.

Pursuing and achieving your best life is part of the journey to truly becoming a highly effective leader. Fulfilling this journey requires that we recognize and remove self-sabotage from our lives. Forces of self-sabotage tell us constantly that achieving better and greater in our lives is an impossible—or even unreasonable—pursuit.

It can be argued that the people who are living their best lives are the authors of books we read for tips and advice, leaders or founders of the companies you work for or wealthy philanthropists who shape the world into a better place.

Each of these are acts of leadership. For the very small percentage of people who are truly living their best life, they began by making the decision to ignore the internal betrayer in their minds that constantly told them to stop pursuing greater in their lives.

Your best life may be measured in financial wealth, independence, happiness, or some other way. Regardless of how you measure it, you know what you need in order to achieve your goals. Even more, you know that you are not living that life today.

Although there are a myriad of outside forces we can point to that stop us from deciding to pursue greater, no external betrayal can be blamed for self-doubt and low self-efficacy.

These are self-inflicted wounds. This is the sabotage that hurts the worst.

No leadership guide is complete without turning the mirror inward and encouraging leaders to demand more from themselves with the same vigor that they demand from others. Checking our own internal drive is the start to truly tapping into your potential for operating as the best version of yourself.

Checking the negative forces within yourself and removing them as obstacles for leading and pursuing greater carries the following benefits:

IT GIVES YOU CLARITY AND STRENGTHENS DISCERNMENT

Many leaders fail to see sabotage because their vision, heart and mind are clouded with barriers that we allow to persist in our lives. Getting your internal house in order is like removing a light beam from your eye. It clears your vision, sharpens your discernment, and helps you distinguish between the pollution and purpose for your life.

IT GIVES YOU VISION

Being able to see and having vision are two different things. Seeing enables you to visually conceive that which is before you. Having vision is an ability that allows leaders to behold the unseen, predict the future and make present-day decisions as though they were operating in that future. Moreover, having vision is a choice.

While describing his life, my brother aptly explained in two sentences why some people choose to not live with vision: "When you're poor it's impossible to spend time working on the future. All I have the ability to do is survive in the now." Having vision has never been about poverty or wealth. It's always about what we allow for ourselves. Leaders must allow themselves to have vision.

IT GIVES YOU SIMPLICITY

There is a reason the desks of really effective leaders are often impeccably clean. The reason is because the things that make it to their desks are the things that truly matter. Our internal lives should be the same way. Once a leader achieves clarity and vision, they maintain it by being highly selective about the things they allow into their lives. The kind of simplicity that can be achieved when leaders clean their internal house can be sweeping. It can impact the people you associate with and the way you spend your time and money.

FINALLY, IT MAKES LIFE LIGHTER

Your life can be quite heavy. Carrying around the weight of low self-esteem and other people's problems doesn't help. Ridding these things from your life won't make the journey towards greater any less challenging, but it will certainly make it less burdensome.

The following chapters will help you identify and remove the forces of self-sabotage that's holding you back. Within these chapters are the strategies for breaking down the mental barriers that keep your life stagnant, and tell you to be content with mediocrity.

It's time to break free from what's holding you back. It's time to join the small number of achievers who have defeated self-sabotage, and as a result are living their best lives.

THE BRIEF

Self-sabotage defined:

- Self-sabotage is behavior that creates problems in one's life that undermine or interfere with longstanding goals.
- Self-sabotage barricades us into lives of mediocrity, or worse, poverty.
- Self-sabotage is anchored in self-doubt, low self-confidence or low self-efficacy.

Ultimate goal of self-sabotage: to stop us from living our very best lives.

How we know self-sabotage is rampant:

- Most people die without realizing their life's dreams. Those who do decided to ignore the forces of self-sabotage.
- Pursuing and achieving your best life is part of the journey to truly becoming a highly effective leader.

Benefits of identifying and removing negative forces that lead to self-sabotage:

- Greater clarity and discernment
- Greater vision
- Greater simplicity
- A lighter, less burdensome life

CHAPTER FIFTEEN

IS COMPLACENCY DRIVING YOU TO SELF-SABOTAGE?

Comfort is alluring. It's what we strive to have in our lives. It is also something to be cherished and preserved.

But like most things, comfort is also a two-sided coin. On one side of the coin—the side we reference most often—is consistency, predictability and met needs.

On the other side of the coin—the side rarely spoken about—is complacency.

Complacency has little to do with one's present circumstances and everything to do with one's internal feelings about the things they have in their life.

By definition, complacency is being pleased with oneself—especially one's merit or situation. The complacent are typically so self-satisfied that they are blinded to opportunities to achieve greater and the dangers that threaten their present circumstances.

It is the complacent leader who willingly sabotages their own pursuits for better in hopes of preserving the present.

The present is a fleeting thing. It passes in an instant, as change and transition are all around us.

To cope, the complacent leader justifies why they choose to abort, ignore or dismiss the pursuit for greater. They tell themselves that they are fine where they are, or that the required effort is simply not worth the risk of harm to their reputation.

What if I fail? and *what if things don't pan out?* are the questions that loom subconsciously and anchor them to the present.

Resistance to the risks associated with pursuing greater is present in all of our lives. It takes many forms and manifests itself in different ways, depending on the leader.

However, what is consistent are the lost opportunities. Complacent leaders consistently miss out on opportunities to become more innovative because acquiring a new skill requires being exposed to the discomfort of not knowing.

They miss out on growth and expansion because both of these represent the need to build capacity beyond what they know and can manage in the present.

And lastly, the complacent leader consistently misses out of new streams of revenue and income. As economies change, these leaders have a hard time adjusting to remain relevant.

Conquering the complacency in each of us requires that all leaders come to terms with their own susceptibility to this internal betrayer.

These anecdotes, organized in ascending order, hone in on our penchant for using complacency to sabotage ourselves. The more familiar the anecdote sounds to your personal life, the greater the chances that you've found yourself on the spectrum of susceptibility to self-sabotage.

"I HAVE A BETTER LIFE THAN MY PARENTS HAD AT THIS AGE."

Our parents have dreams for us that outweigh what they've achieved in their lives. They wish for us to own things, and to not be renters. Some wish that their children earn college degrees if they themselves never reached that milestone in their life. Others simply encourage their children to not have children before they are of a responsible age. As a result, some people are just okay living a life that's only a little bit better than their parents. The problem with this is that our parents' dreams for us often pale in comparison to the dreams we've held for ourselves since we were little children.

"I HAVE A WELL-PAYING JOB."

Some of you work for a corporation or large company that has given you good benefits, a vice president title, and a salary that allows you to live in a gated or exclusive community. Your needs are met. Your retirement plans are on track. Your children go to a good school. You're living a very comfortable life. This comfort, in many ways, is a barrier to your desire to achieve more. You view the pursuit for greater as too risky. Even when faced with the fact that your prospects for promotion will diminish with time, or that you will likely never earn more than your prescribed salary schedule, you surrender to the present and forfeit any notion of pursuing expansion.

"BETTER IS NOT FOR ME."

The fallacy that "better is for someone else" looms large in your mind. Having or being more is something reserved for those who own companies we work for, or those who mentor or lead us. This is not true.

This belief is predicated on the myth that each person's destiny is predetermined. For example, if your family is poor, then you too must be destined for poverty. If your parents raised you in the projects, then you too are destined to live in public housing. If you are from a broken home, then your life too must be broken.

We are each endowed with opportunities to impact and shape our lives. We choose to make good grades. We choose to attend college. We choose to be great. We also choose to not be great. These choices are our own.

Believing that you are born with a life destined for under-achievement and mediocrity is the kind of thinking that fuels generational curses.

Like all things, complacency can be overcome. Doing so requires a keen and relentless focus on the "why" that drives your pursuits for greater. Those "whys"—whether they are to be a good role model, change an industry or provide for those you love—comprise the fuel that powers your leadership.

Find ways to keep your drivers top of mind, even as your prosperity and promotions increase. Refuse to grow content spending the rest of your life standing where you are.

As a strategy, avoiding complacency requires refusing to become consumed with how others see you. This is not why you lead. So, the views and opinions of others should not be why you stop leading.

If one of your leadership pursuits doesn't pan out, make sure the pursuit was worth it by seeking the desires of your heart, not the approval of others. In doing so, you will become resilient. If you fail, there might be laughter. There might even be mockery from others. But when you refuse to let the approval of others become your leadership fuel, you will always be able to get up, dust yourself off and continue your pursuit fully confident that your failure today has sharpened you for the journey tomorrow.

As a leader, there is always the likelihood of failure. However, if all of your pursuits align with the things that fill you with the most gratitude, you're less likely to become debilitated by the sting of failure.

THE BRIEF

Complacency defined:

Complacency is being pleased with oneself—especially one's merit or situation. The complacent are typically so self-satisfied that they are blinded to opportunities to achieve greater and the dangers that threaten their present circumstances.

Lies complacent leaders tell themselves to justify self-sabotage:

- I am fine with where I am in life.
- Pursuing better is simply not worth the risk to my reputation.

Common refrains of self-sabotage by complacency:

- "I have a better life than my parents had at this age."
- "I have a well-paying job."
- "Better is not for me."

Leadership techniques:

- Avoid complacency by developing ways to keep your "why's" for achieving better at the forefront of your mind.
- Refuse to become consumed with how others perceive you.

CHAPTER SIXTEEN

IS FEAR OF SUCCESS DRIVING YOU TO SELF-SABOTAGE?

F ear is a potent driver for self-sabotage. I've seen it creep into people's lives and rob them of their opportunities to better their lives.

Not to pick on athletes, but if you watch closely, you'll witness the impact fear can have on a life. Take athletes who enter the NFL Draft, or openly make plans to play some professional sport. These transitions are littered with stories of athletes who just can't seem to get out of their own way as they try to close multimillion dollar deals and elevate their status and influence.

You know the stories well. An athlete is found recklessly increasing their use of drugs as draft day nears. They might send irresponsible tweets as they enter final negotiations for a major endorsement deal. They may even engage in violent fights and scuffles that lead to arrests that threaten to dash their hopes of striking it large.

Many of you may call these acts irresponsible missteps from young, impressionable athletes. But I see something altogether different: Fear of success causing the person to self-sabotage.

It is my opinion that these acts are classic attempts to sabotage the future for sheer fear of becoming a multimillionaire with influence and to avoid the accountability and responsibility that comes with it. As overt as these acts are, I believe the silent undercurrent driving the self-sabotage is an unspoken and subconscious fear of greater.

This kind of fear can seep into our own lives. We rarely, if ever, speak of it. Achieving greater is daunting for some. Consider the outlook of someone who has only known poverty all of their lives, or who has grown accustomed to struggling and hustling to make it. Then, honestly assess the unfamiliarity and weight that comes with reaching new heights. The very thought can be petrifying and can mobilize fear that clouds your mind and judgment.

We are all susceptible to the effects fear can have on our ability to pursue greater. That fear compels us to justify why we deny ourselves opportunities for better, in exchange for preserving what we already have.

This justification is an act of sabotage against ourselves.

Here is how it sounds:

"I AM FINE WHERE I AM."

I have kids. I have a family to take care of. I have too much going on to think about starting or doing anything differently in my life. Starting a business and pursuing more is a pipe dream. I have real obligations right in front of me.

Every big achiever and influencer known to the world today and throughout history had to begin somewhere. And, they had to begin someday—despite their present circumstances. Today could be your day.

Conceding your dreams to your present day reality is tantamount to quitting—giving up on your inheritance and giving up on the journey to becoming highly successful.

However, the fearful leader may not see things this way. They tell themselves or have friends who tell them that to make it in life, one needs only to marry up. Or the message is that pursuing dreams at any age is simply too risky. They might say taking risks is something they should not be willing to expose their children to or risk losing their job for.

Sounds pretty reasonable on its face. But it is an incredibly flawed life to lead, and one that is at odds with the practices and beliefs of leaders who overcome self sabotage, and achieve their best life.

"I AM OKAY WITH ONLY PURSUING MY NEXT PAYCHECK."

Coming to terms with the need to plan for the future and set resources aside for a rainy day is seen as a luxury for some. The needs of people who only live for the next paycheck often find themselves on a treadmill of dependency to their workplace and their own resourcefulness.

If your dependency is on the workplace, then living paycheck-to-paycheck is a common refrain used to describe one's financial situation. The reality here is that after paying one's bills and taking care of immediate needs, they find themselves with little to no money to donate, plan, tithe or set aside for an emergency.

If the dependence is on their own resourcefulness, then they try to find a way to piece together enough money to fill the gap from paying for the needs of the day—striving to earn a few extra dollars for tomorrow.

Examples of this hustle look like attempts to look for easy, and sometimes unethical, financial gain. You have a job, but look for ways to not pay your mortgage or rent, or have others pay for it.

People with this mindset may even opt to find someone willing to sell food stamps or government assistance cards to avoid taxes on grocery items. There is always another hustle and the hustles are seen as dire needs of survival—not as mere plays for another buck. The reality, however, is that short-term wins never outweigh investments made to set up long-term gains.

There is so much more to life than this. But for those who tell themselves lies that lock them into prisons of poverty and sameness, they have allowed fear to become the thief who steals their opportunities for greatness.

Overcoming the debilitating effects fear can have on you requires that you discover the power of joy. Leaders must choose to be joyful in all of their pursuits. Being joyful about the journey as you walk the path towards success has a heart-changing ability for leaders who once would have been consumed and defined by whatever the outcome of the journey held for them.

If the path is for more money, enjoy the journey and refuse to let momentary fluctuations in your money define you. If the path is excelling at a particular sport—play every game with a joy that exudes from every move and don't emphasize the score. If the path is for promotion, advancement or whatever form of greater you can imagine, find joy in the journey.

Joy is more than happiness.

Joy is the ability to let yourself become consumed with elation about the things you are passionate about doing. With joy, the doing matters so much more than the resources, money or fame that results from the activities. You can't "do" fame or money. You can't "do" celebrity or rich. Because of this, your joys mustn't be buried in these things.

Like fear, joy is a choice. Choose joy and choke fear from your life and leadership.

THE BRIEF

Common refrains for self-sabotage by fear:

- "I am fine where I am."
- "I am okay with only pursuing my next paycheck."

Leadership techniques: Overcoming self-sabotage by fear of success requires finding joy.

Joy is more than happiness. Joy is the ability to let yourself to become consumed with elation about the things you are passionate about doing.

CHAPTER SEVENTEEN

IS SELF-DOUBT DRIVING YOU TO SELF-SABOTAGE?

Belief in oneself is an important, yet very fragile, element to our ability to lead. It is the cornerstone of both self-esteem—our perception of ourselves—and self-efficacy—the extent of our belief in our ability to achieve.

Both self-esteem and self-efficacy, when harnessed, can provide you with the fuel you need to live powerful lives and become powerful leaders.

When belief is not guarded, it can easily get crushed, stolen or unintentionally given away by leaders. Understanding the impact this can have to one's ability to lead can best be understood through the lens of someone sitting in the county fair dunking booth.

The person sitting in the booth appears confident. They humor the crowd, making faces and taunting the person trying to dunk them. The crowd indulges, creating the appearance that the subject in the booth has influence and control.

This could not be further from the truth. Hit the target and the subject tumbles through the platform into the water-filled bottom.

In real life, a leader with vulnerable belief in themselves is in the same predicament as the person in the dunking booth. If people learn the right buttons to push, the leader can be controlled, manipulated and sunken at a moment's notice.

To remain in control of your life's journey, and avoid it being hijacked by those with ill intent, leverage the belief you have in yourself to lead. Doing so can help you channel an inner independence and will provide you clarity in your decision-making. Leading in this way makes your ability to be effective a central aim, not the satisfaction of others.

When leaders stop believing in themselves, the common symptom is self-doubt. Self-doubt is best defined by an absence or lack of confidence in one's ability to be effective.

Self-doubt has a voice and an insistent script littered with language of limiting and defeating effect. The two most common lies self-doubt tells leaders are that life is set up to ensure failure and that which you seek to accomplish simply can't be done.

"LIFE IS SET UP AGAINST ME."

Life certainly is not fair. This is a truism. But to live a life that embodies this sentiment is a life that's set up with the expectation that failure is inevitable. There are -isms in all walks of life. Racism is alive and healthy in the world. So is sexism, ageism, oppression and disenfranchisement that truly make achievement more difficult for some than others. But these difficulties plague all of us at some level (albeit to varying degrees), thus making characteristics like hard work, resilience and persistence essential for achieving extraordinary success.

People who live a life with the statement, "Life is not fair" as a cornerstone have filled their tanks with excuses. "I am too tired." "I am too poor." "I don't have the tools to make things happen." "No one will listen to me." "I can't get a loan." And the excuse of all excuses from people who let self-doubt rule their lives is, "No one wants to help me." When self-doubt consumes a person's life, blaming others for their failures becomes a daily pursuit. The consequence of this is a life of dependency on others.

"I CAN'T DO IT."

When my wife and I opened our home to our seven-year-old niece, one of the things we had to teach her was the difference between can't and won't. She would often ask for things by saying, "Can you do xyz, for me?" as opposed to "Will you do x,y,z for me?" Albeit subtle, the misunderstanding of these words can be consequential when it comes to one's perceived ability to achieve their dreams or get anything done in life.

You see, "can't" is a matter of ability. "Won't" is a matter of willingness. People who believe they "can't" achieve their best life have convinced themselves that they "can't" achieve more. But the real matter is that they truly lack the "will" to seek and work for more. Having the will to achieve better is a solvable matter. Lacking the ability to achieve better, not so much.

People who believe that they "can't" achieve success are quite diverse. Some work at lucrative jobs and have college or graduate degrees, while others might live from paycheck to paycheck, or hustle for the next dollar. However, the common thread that binds all of them together is a feeling that they "can't" achieve more.

A common refrain heard here is, "Even though I have these degrees, I believe I am overqualified to seek a promotion." Or, "I hate my job, but no one else will hire me so I won't waste my time looking for anything better." Another excuse is "Times have changed so much that people are no longer looking to hire or do business with someone my age." The level of debilitation from those who "can't" is palpable.

People stop wanting to be associated with people who believe they simply "can't" achieve success because, over time, they become doubters of everyone's dreams, not just their own.

Self-doubt is a liar. It preys on people who have lost belief in themselves. It causes leaders to sabotage themselves by refusing to try.

As a practical matter, leaders don't win every time they swing, and sometimes disappointment is the only trophy won by those who are audacious and fall short. But another thing is also true: letting self-doubt deter you is a sure way to fail every time.

THE BRIEF

Unguarded belief in oneself can easily get crushed, stolen or unintentionally given away by leaders.

Common refrains of self-doubt:

- "Life is set up against me."
- "I can't do it."

Examples of how self-doubt sounds:

- "Even though I have these degrees, I believe I am overqualified to seek a promotion."
- "I hate my job, but no one else will hire me so why look for anything better?"
- "Times have changed so much that people are no longer looking to hire or do business with someone of a certain age."

Leadership techniques:

Confronting self-doubt requires that leaders understand that it is a liar.

CHAPTER EIGHTEEN

THE MOST POWERFUL WEAPON FOR REMOVING SELF-SABOTAGE FROM YOUR LIFE

Throughout life, our experiences with others create openings for self-sabotage to enter our lives—whether it's the low confidence that develops as a result of being in a series of abusive relationships or the idea that we are not valuable that results from growing up around parents who speak negatively about your character.

The relationships we have with others and our collective experiences with failure and success create portals for self-sabotage to rob us of our greatness.

We are all vulnerable to self-sabotage. I am not an exception.

In 2014, I had what I thought was an amazing idea. I decided to explore starting a business that would provide home grocery delivery services to neighborhoods across the U.S.

This creative idea was seared into my heart. I burned with enthusiasm every time I thought about the potential for this business. I envisioned the day I could provide jobs to young delivery people who took pride in providing a service of value to their community. I envisioned providing a platform that allowed moms to shop for other moms. I also envisioned the impact my technology could have in revolutionizing the way we shopped, forever.

I jumped to action. I developed a business plan, identified funding sources and established a start-up budget. I vetted the idea with trusted advisers. When all systems appeared to agree with pursuing this idea, I selected a research firm to discover the size of the appetite customers held for such an experience.

The researcher I interviewed shared that one of their clients had a similar idea. She talked about the trials he experienced trying to pull an idea like mine together and get it off the ground. She said it sounded as though he had a lot of challenges. What she said about her client's difficulties stuck with me.

I went home and talked with my wife about the idea and the conversation I had with the researcher. My wife instantly pointed to those challenges, highlighting that I already had a lot of irons in the fire and that the risk of this new venture could potentially be too much to assume at the time.

I then started to counsel with myself, telling myself everything contrary to my original belief that this was a great idea. I told myself that the idea was faulty. I told myself that I knew nothing about the grocery industry and held no credibility to be effective. I told myself that I would fail.

After counseling with myself long enough, I decided to pull the plug on the idea completely. I simply did not believe that I could do it. I didn't think that I could succeed. I saw myself as incapable.

That same year, in a suburb of my hometown, another leader had the same idea. His name is Bill Smith. He is a high school dropout from a family of entrepreneurs. Despite his educational background, he was a confident leader. He believed in his abilities. He saw himself as an achiever.

As I sat on the sidelines, I watched as Bill's upstart company that delivered groceries to families across the country grew into a giant over the next three years.

Bill's company was named Shipt. You may have heard of it. In 2017, it was purchased by Target Corp. for $550,000,000.

In 2019, I had the fortune of attending a meeting with Brian Cornell, Chairman and CEO at Target Corp. In that meeting he shared that he was drawn to Shipt because he believed in its ability to be a platform that allowed moms to shop for other moms. He thought that idea was revolutionary.

Sound familiar? Before I allowed self-sabotage to control my destiny, I once thought the same thing.

My self-sabotage was indeed quite costly. It costs me a chance at earning $550,000,000. I allowed my past struggles in business to sway my confidence, while Bill refused to fear failure and held to his belief in himself as an effective leader.

I believe that at the time, the only thing that distinguished me and Bill Smith was the way we viewed ourselves as leaders.

Self-image is a powerful force. It looms large when it comes to us truly believing in our ability to realize greatness in our lives. It is so powerful that I believe that it alone is the assassin to self-sabotage.

Only when we start seeing ourselves as leaders who are effective, successful, confident, bold, and courageous will we begin allowing ourselves to experience greatness.

In other words, we all do things for ourselves—and *to* ourselves—that are consistent with the way we see ourselves.

Change your self-image and change your personal relationship with greatness.

Slaying self-sabotage, thus changing your self image, begins with looking in the mirror. It requires that we discover where the origins of our self-image reside—with ourselves, with others or with our past. It also requires that we ask if the image we see in the mirror is what others project on us or if that image is the one we hold without bias.

It takes a lot of work to dissolve the impact of negative experiences, relationships and perceptions of authority figures.

For example, when parents call their children dumb or tell them that they will never achieve anything in life, those words can take root in the hearts of those children because they value the opinions and authority of their parents. When people experience struggles financially, they can easily start seeing themselves as impoverished or as a failure. In cases where people are never allowed to truly experience triumph—be it because of abuse, poverty or bullying—growing up with a self-image that says success is something that can only be given to them by others can become their reality.

Don't allow other people or your past experiences to dictate how you see yourself. In doing so, you also are refusing to let your past dictate your future.

Assassinating self-sabotage requires that we start seeing ourselves as people who overcome, win and finish.

WHEN YOU SEE YOURSELF AS A FIGHTER, YOU WILL OVERCOME

Life guarantees that we will face challenges and difficulties. When these challenging times happen, those moments can be frightening and filled with uncertainty. Your ability to overcome these times requires that you see yourself as a fighter. People who try to block your ability to overcome will plant seeds of fear in you. They will decry your ability to survive the loss of a job or the challenges that come with starting a new business. But the reality is that those who want to negatively impact your self image are themselves afraid of uncertainty and challenge.

Don't let their fears become yours.

Seeing yourself as a person who can overcome anything will change the way you perceive challenges. Those who overcome see challenges as opportunities for growth and development. They also see loss as platforms for lessons that prepare them for future successes. When you see yourself this way, you literally see differently. And what you see will affect the way you walk in times of difficulty.

WHEN YOU SEE YOURSELF AS A WINNER, YOU WIN

You are a winner. Read that sentence as many times as it takes. Internalize it. Believe that you are designed to win.

Along this journey, you will find yourself down. Refuse to let those moments define how you see yourself. Don't let the failings experienced along your journey trick you into seeing yourself as a failure.

Don't allow those in authority in your life trick you into believing you're incapable of leadership. When they do try to diminish your confidence to lead, know that they are only projecting their lack of confidence in their ability to lead on you.

Don't accept anything from anyone that's less than a proclamation that you are valuable, capable and effective.

Winning at anything in life requires confronting challenges and adversities. It requires that we invest in what we're good at—thus sharpening our skills and abilities at every turn. It also requires that we find ways to make those around us better.

But most importantly, being a winner requires improved eyesight. Winners see differently. They see every bump in the road, every lost battle—and even every victory—as preparation for the fulfillment of their greatness. They don't remain fixated on those tough times in life. Even more, they refuse to let those down times define who they are, or shape who they will become.

These are the ways of winners. Start slaying the self-sabotage that seeks to limit your life by seeing yourself as a winner.

WHEN YOU SEE YOURSELF AS A FINISHER, YOU WILL FINISH

There is nothing more satisfying to self-sabotage—or sabotage in its traditional form—than causing you to quit.

When you quit anything in life, it affirms the lies self-sabotage plants in your heart and provides fuel for the forces of self-sabotage to repeatedly attack your will.

If you wrestle with being a finisher, remind yourself that no one ever wins at anything when they quit.

Refusing to finish is quitting.

I am the first to declare that finishing is difficult. But I also realize that finishing is a discipline. Discipline is a set of activities, that when consistently executed, creates traits that become valuable in all areas of life.

For instance, working out and eating healthy takes discipline. But those who achieve this discipline enjoy more energy, athleticism, and strength that benefits their entire life.

Becoming a finisher requires that you become a disciple of completion. Sharpening your ability to complete everything you start will also make you more reliable. People will begin investing in your abilities and honoring your commitment to completion with promotion. Self-sabotage will have you believe that you are unreliable and unsteady. Finishers see themselves differently.

Finishers are also trustworthy. People translate a commitment to seeing things through to the end as keeping your word. Finishers become leaders that people turn to and trust with their most precious assets and responsibilities. More importantly, finishers trust themselves.

Finishers are also thoughtful and pragmatic. Because they are disciples of completion, they give great thought to their commitments. They ensure that the things they commit to doing are realistic and sensible. In this way, finishers are hard to fool and turn down more opportunities than they accept.

Lastly, finishers are executives. In other words, they are doers who possess the ability and influence to empower others to also do. Executives own their journeys to greatness and are generous about allowing others around them to participate and contribute to building their destiny.

So, next time the voice of self-sabotage whispers—or screams—that you are not worthy or too weak, tell it to shut up. Tell the forces of self-sabotage that it doesn't know who you are, or that you are designed for greatness.

Next time you look in the mirror, I want you to truly see yourself—not what self-sabotage wants you to see.

See yourself. See a person who always overcomes. See a winner. See a finisher. When you do, the realities of your life will begin aligning with that image and will unlock all of the benefits that come with having a positive self-image.

THE BRIEF

Having a positive self-image destroys self-sabotage. Having a positive self-image renders the lies self-sabotage tell us ineffective.

When you change your self-image, you change your access to the greatness that awaits your life and leadership.

How to change your self-image:

- Refuse to allow those in authority to diminish your confidence to lead
- Refuse to let your past dictate your future
- Refuse to accept anything from anyone that's less than declaring you as effective, valuable and capable

Leadership Techniques:

Assassinating self-sabotage requires that you see yourself as a person who can overcome, win and finish.

- **People who overcome** possess the ability to transcend the difficulties of life and all of its challenges.
- **Winners believe** that the entirety of their life journey prepares them for greatness
- **Finishers are disciples of completion.** They harness the discipline of getting things done.

WHEN SABOTAGE
GETS THE BEST
OF YOU

———

CHAPTER NINETEEN

SURVIVING SABOTAGE REQUIRES LEARNING TO MANAGE DISAPPOINTMENT

D isappointment looms large in every leader's life. Nobody wants to talk about it, yet we all have battled with our fair share of it.

Not talking about disappointment does a disservice to emerging leaders everywhere. Minimizing it as a trivial matter is even worse. I've seen leaders do both. In doing so, we miss opportunities to leverage the lessons learned from disappointment to help others prepare to deal with it as they develop into effective leaders.

Disappointment happens when that trusted colleague or friend leads you astray or betrays your trust. It happens when the potential client you've been meeting with for months reneges on your deal in the eleventh hour. It happens when your strategies fail to realize your objectives. It also happens when your career stalls despite the expectation that you should be advancing.

We've all been there.

It is in these moments of sabotage that we can feel the most defeated and vulnerable. We might believe we've failed ourselves and those who look to us to always win, triumph and effectively navigate our way to our desired ends.

Unfortunately, that's not how things always go.

For many of us, our reality is closer to believing we will meet revenue projections—even hiring staff before the money is realized—only to find ourselves falling short, having to delay payroll or worse, fire employees.

Or maybe our reality is believing in a business partner with the kind of enthusiasm that causes us to make wild investments in their abilities, only to be let down by their inability to meet the expectations they originally sold us at the beginning of the relationship.

To hone in on why disappointment is so pervasive in our lives—while addressing it is so evasive—we must understand that disappointment exists as a result of something falling short of its promise.

Every day we are promised things. Our employees promise us that they will arrive to work on time every day. Our children promise us that they will always make the right decision when faced with illicit temptations. Our spouses promise us that they will always be patient with us.

When you awake in the morning, each of us can expect to be promised something. When those promises are not realized, the way we respond to the shortcomings can open the door for disappointment to enter our lives.

I'm sure many of you are fully aware of the power of promise. We make promises all the time to would-be consumers. We've all seen the commercials for sports drinks that promise to enhance our athletic performance, or the fad diets that tout unbelievable results in weeks. There are endless car commercials that show a luxury automobile in front of a modern million-dollar home to make the point that purchasing the car will make you feel rich.

The realities are always a bit different than what the commercials promise. You are still exhausted after a few miles of running despite drinking the sports drink. The meals that come with the diet plans are not as tasty or satisfying as they look on television, and buying the luxury car resulted in such a financial hit that you feel less rich than before you bought it.

The space that exists in between what we expect and what we actually receive in life is where disappointment lives.

Managing disappointment requires that we identify and control how we assign expectations to things in our lives.

At its core, disappointment is all about you. Its presence in our lives has less to do with any outside forces and more to do with your process for placing your expectations.

To fully appreciate this, let's examine the construction of the word disappointment. The root of the word is appoint, which means designate or assign. The prefix "Dis" is latin for apart or away. The *dis* in disappointment refers to something being displaced or ill-appointed.

So, if disappointment is all about how you place your expectations, the key to managing disappointment—and removing it from your life—rests in your ability to identify the things that influence your expectations.

To help you pinpoint the true manager of your expectations, here are a few prompts that commonly lead people to having ill-appointed expectations:

THE LIVES OF OTHER PEOPLE

Often we look to the lives of others and take the cues they provide us to draw conclusions about our lives. We often look curiously at the business practices of successful business owners and tell ourselves that if only we do what they did, we would be successful. We look to the marriages of others, and convince ourselves that the things that works for them will work for us. We look to stories and myths told on television and other media about the glamour of entrepreneurship, then set expectations that lead us to dismiss the hard work and risks required to grow any venture.

Allowing the lives of other people to assign our expectations is almost certain to lead to disappointment. One rule makes this true: The journey of others is not your journey. The lives of others is often an inaccurate and unfair rubric for assessing where your own expectations should be assigned.

FANTASY AND IMAGINATION

Hollywood has built an entire industry on fantasy and playwrights have used fictional stories to elicit real life sympathy and emotional investment into the wondrous creations of their minds for decades. People flock to theaters, tune in on their televisions or purchase books to root for the defeat of the Dark Side with every Star Wars installation or cheer for their favorite house on Game of Thrones as though their lives were real.

It's fun. It's fantastic. And of course, it's all fake.

In terms of the entertainment we enjoy, they are fun and for the most part, harmless. However, they provide a context for understanding the harm that could be done when we become the authors of fantasies in our lives, and use those fantasies to convince ourselves of things that dispute truth and reality.

It is in these instances that imagination and fantasy can lead to disappointment.

It is in these instances that we find people willing themselves to continue to trust business partners even after signs and evidence loudly indicate that they are not upholding their end of the bargain or acting in the best interest of your joint venture.

Fantasy can make us ignore the fact that we probably should end the friendship with someone who constantly leads us into trouble or applies unfair blame.

But the effects of fantasy, or the ill appointment of expectation, doesn't necessarily have to involve others. Sometimes, they are solo acts of self-inflicted wounds. Examples of this see business owners clinging to the fantasy of themselves as independent bosses who are millionaires—even though the reality is that the business is failing and plummeting fast. The fantasy this person has built has made it difficult to loose themselves of the sinking ship, and thus they cling to it until their financial death so that the fantasy they've built can persist.

Manage the fantasies in your life. Avoid basing matters of reality on imagination. Doing this is one way to reduce disappointment.

LACK OF INFORMATION

Expectations can be compared to employees in a business. When they are well-placed, the employees will satisfy the demands of the role. When they are not, the employee will likely underperform.

There have been times when I've made hires or assigned responsibilities to people and inadvertently put them in an unfair position to underperform—the duties just didn't quite align with their strengths. The result was always the same: unfulfilled and unmet potential.

Likewise, having displaced expectations commonly leads to expectations not being fully met or ones that fall short of its full promise.

In some of these situations, I simply made a poor personnel decision. At other times, I just didn't know enough about the person before hiring or promoting them.

Whichever the case, I found myself operating without sufficient information, basing my expectations on what I didn't know. Put another way, I allowed insufficient information to assign my expectations.

As a result, the employees let me down, failed to realize their full potential and ultimately failed to meet my expectations. This is common in management, but also in life.

In life, we sometimes find ourselves selecting friends, significant others, confidants and employers without fully understanding the person we're choosing to engage with.

Despite this lack of knowledge, we dive in fully, fill our minds with expectations of trust, integrity, reliability, protection and dependability—all while not fully knowing if the people are capable of meeting those responsibilities and promises.

Operating with lack of information is not only reckless, but it can also be dangerous. We see these dangers when those we love choose the wrong spouse or significant other. Or, we might see it when peers throw themselves headlong into relationships where they end up trusting people pretending to be someone they are not, called "catfish". However, true to the framework for understanding disappointment, the disappointment has more to do with you than any other outside or opposing force.

For example, in almost every catfish scenario, the victim fills in the gaps of information with imaginative ideations that make up for the gaps of information and inaccuracies. The victims tell themselves that the person's car just always has mechanical problems while trying to understand why opportunities to meet always fall apart at the last minute, or they might convince themselves that the object of their affection really loves and cares for them despite being married to someone else. These lies help the victims feel better about their misplaced expectations, and as a result, feel justified to remain in the poor and unproductive relationship.

Whether it be in management, leadership or our personal lives, the longer we remain in these relationships, the more harm they cause and the harder it becomes to end them. As a simple maxim, be slow to hire and quick to fire. This approach will help you avoid a lot of pain and hurt.

The first step in managing disappointment in and around your life is discovering what is assigning your expectations.

Expecting to prevail over sabotage every time is fantasy. Trusting every person completely with your work, treasure or heart without fear of betrayal is living without complete knowledge of those you entrust. Expecting your leadership to always end in heroic bliss like it does for the authors and mentors we follow is looking to the lives of others to define how our lives should work.

Start taking your expectations out of these banks and you will see an immediate reduction in the amount of disappointment in your life.

THE BRIEF

Dissecting disappointment:

The *dis* in disappointment refers to something being displaced or ill-appointed.

Managing disappointment requires that we identify and manage the things in our lives that we allow to assign our expectations.

Things we commonly allow to assign our expectations:

- The lives of other people
- Fantasy and imagination
- Lack of information

Leadership technique: The first step in managing disappointment in your life is discovering what is assigning your expectations. Once you identify the true managers of your expectations, you can then choose to stop investing your hopes in the places that continue to let you down.

FINAL WORDS
FOR LEADERS

CHAPTER TWENTY

LEARNING TO SURVIVE SABOTAGE LEADS TO IMPROVED LEADERSHIP

At this point in the book, one thing should be glaringly clear: A study of sabotage is a study of leadership.

You've been given perhaps the most comprehensive set of weaponry for overcoming sabotage that you'll find in one place. Simultaneously, you've been given the tools you need to become a more effective leader.

All leaders—in every industry, life and organization type—aim to achieve legacy-defining, transformative change in the lives of those they serve, and the organizations they lead. As difficult as it is to climb this mountain time and time again, sabotage inevitably strikes to make the tasks at hand even more challenging.

Until now, you were defenseless. That is no longer the case. The insights you now have into the behavior that is sabotage—betrayal, theft and deceit—will help you plan for the inevitable and spend more time pursuing your leadership journey to improve the lives of others, ultimately leading to greater things in your life.

There are leaders of all walks of life who simply believe in doing what is right and helping others achieve better.

I have a special word of encouragement for each of you, as you venture forward as leaders prepared to rise above sabotage and achieve new leadership heights:

Corporate leaders, you stand in the shadows of giants. Those giants are your legendary predecessors and the founders of your companies. Your organizations are large and have influence that runs deep and reaches wide. I challenge you to not shrink in the shadows of those who came before you.

The stakes are high. Your leadership pursuits promise to give you your own legacy, and operatives of sabotage will plot to stop you from fulfilling your promise. I often remind leaders that despite the size of your corporations, they were founded by an individual or small group of leaders who faced challenges, and rose above them. Become a student of the nuances of sabotage, and prepare daily to chart your own legacy.

Political leaders, your decisions affect a multitude of people. Your platform is massive, and your influence requires supreme discipline and wisdom. The stakes are high. Preserve the purity of your job by refusing to let sabotage turn you against your colleagues.

Your leadership platform is the best there is. Your only job each day is thinking of ways to improve the lives of others. When agents of sabotage pull you away from this mission, they want you to belittle your colleagues and work in ways that are destructive. The net effect of this is a diminished public discourse and the failing of public service. Guard yourself against sabotage.

Entrepreneurial leaders, be bold. Be so innovative that your presence challenges tradition. It is your inventions, products and services that provide the force that creates new industries and disrupts others.

Agents of sabotage will tell you that you can't succeed. They will tell you to doubt yourself. They will show you fear and tell you that it awaits you on the other side of your pursuit. Don't believe it. Dare to be audacious. The future depends on it. The stakes are high.

Finally, for **leaders with no title**—you believe in greater for yourself and better for those who look to you. Your life is an example of what can happen when you lead boldly, live your life with character and refuse to let sabotage transform you. Living your best life is one of the greatest honors of any leader. Envision it. Plan for it. Go and get greater.

With your newfound weaponry, sabotage can't stop you.

BIBLIOGRAPHY

"'The Founder' and the Complicated True Story Behind the Founding of McDonald's." Money.com, December 16, 2016. https://money.com/the-founder-mcdonalds-movie-accuracy/.

"A Brief History of Con Edison." A Brief History of Con Edison—electricity. Con Edison. Accessed March 4, 2020. https://web.archive.org/web/20121030164753/ http://www.coned.com/history/electricity.asp.

Abelson, Reed, and Milt Freudenheim. "The Scrushy Mix: Strict and So Lenient." The New York Times, April 20, 2003. https://www.nytimes.com/2003/04/20/business/the-scrushy-mix-strict-and-so-lenient.html.

"Apple FAQ." Apple. Accessed March 4, 2020. https://investor.apple.com/faq/default.aspx.

Bandler, James. "How Bernie Did It." CNNMoney. CNN, April 30, 2009. https://money.cnn.com/2009/04/24/news/newsmakers/madoff.fortune/.

Bates, Daniel. "McDonald's Ray Kroc Cheated the Brothers Who REALLY Started Empire out of $300m." Daily Mail Online. Associated Newspapers, May 5, 2015. https://www.dailymail.co.uk/news/article-3049644/How-McDonald-s-founder-cheated-brothers-REALLY-started-empire-300m-wrote-company-history-left-one-die-heart-failure-barely-millionaire.html.

Berger, Sarah. "Shipt: How This 32-Year-Old High School Dropout Built a Business That Sold to Target for $550 Million." CNBC, October 11, 2018. https://www.cnbc.com/2018/08/10/how-bill-smith-built-shipt-and-sold-it-to-target-for-550-million.html.

"Bernie Madoff." Biography.com, December 10, 2019. https://www.biography.com/crime-figure/bernard-madoff.

"Billy Joel Sues Former Manager for $90 Million." Los Angeles Times. Los Angeles Times, September 26, 1989. https://www.latimes.com/archives/la-xpm-1989-09-26-ca-257-story.html.

Braid, Mary. "Sting's Adviser Jailed for Pounds 6m Theft from Star." The Independent. Independent Digital News and Media, October 22, 2011. https://www.independent.co.uk/news/stings-adviser-jailed-for-pounds-6m-theft-from-star-1578141.html.

"Bullying." Psychology Today. Sussex Publishers. Accessed March 4, 2020. https://www.psychologytoday.com/us/basics/bullying.

Crossman, Matt. "Harding-Kerrigan 20 Years Later: Remembering the Stunning, Life-Changing Attack." Bleacher Report, October 3, 2017. https://bleacherreport.com/articles/1887592-harding-kerrigan-20-years-later-remembering-the-stunning-life-changing-attack.

Edwards, Jim. "Former Apple CEO John Sculley Admits Steve Jobs Never Forgave Him, and He Never Repaired Their Friendship, before Jobs Died." Business Insider, May 27, 2015. https://www.businessinsider.com/john-sculley-admits-steve-jobs-never-forgave-him-before-jobs-died-2015-5.

"Madoff's Victims." Madoff's Victim List . The Wall Street Journal. Accessed March 4, 2020. https://s.wsj.net/public/resources/documents/st_madoff_victims_20081215.html.

Maxwell, John. "Earning Trust (Part 2)." *The John Maxwell Leadership Podcast.* Podcast audio, January 15, 2020.

McCann, David. "Two CFOs Tell a Tale of Fraud at HealthSouth." CFO.com, March 28, 2017. https://www.cfo.com/fraud/2017/03/two-cfos-tell-tale-fraud-healthsouth/.

"Multitasking: Switching Costs." American Psychological Association. Accessed March 4, 2020. https://www.apa.org/research/action/multitask.

Pak, Eudie. "Bernie Madoff's Ponzi Scheme: 6 of His Famous Victims." Biography.com, June 24, 2019. https://www.biography. com/news/bernie-madoff-famous-victims.

Perez, A.J. "Tonya Harding Admits during ABC Special She Heard Talk of Planned Attack." USA Today Sports, January 13, 2018. https://www.usatoday.com/story/sports/ olympics/2018/01/11/tonya-harding-admits-prior-knowledge-nancy-kerrigan-attack-during-abc-special/1023907001/.

"Ray Kroc." Entrepreneur, October 9, 2008. https://www. entrepreneur.com/article/197544.

Rolling Stone. "Rihanna Sues Former Accountants." Rolling Stone, June 25, 2018. https://www.rollingstone.com/music/ music-news/rihanna-sues-former-accountants-242667/.

Rothman, Lily. "Tonya Harding's World Was Nothing Like Nancy Kerrigan's. That Mattered in 1994." Time, December 8, 2017. https://web.archive.org/web/20180719033759/http://time. com/5045902/tonya-harding-nancy-kerrigan-1994/.

Teach, Edward. "'I Should Have Said No.'" CFO.com, June 1, 2009. https://www.cfo.com/human-capital-careers/2009/06/i-should-have-said-no/.

The Editors of Encyclopaedia Britannica. "Bernie Madoff." Encyclopædia Britannica. Encyclopædia Britannica, Inc.,

February 26, 2020. https://www.britannica.com/biography/
Bernie-Madoff.

Zarroli, Jim. "For Madoff Victims, Scars Remain 10 Years Later."
NPR, December 23, 2018. https://www.npr.org/2018/12/23/
678238031/for-madoff-victims-scars-remain-10-years-later.

Made in the USA
Columbia, SC
04 October 2021

46669414R00143